Prince & Little Weird Black Boy Gods
by Scott Woods

BRICK CAVE BOOKS
BrickCaveBooks.com
2018

Prince & Little Weird Black Boy Gods
by Scott Woods

ISBN-13: 978 1 938190 47 6

Published by: Brick Cave Books

Text Design by: Scott Woods & Bob Nelson

Cover Artwork by: Vershawn Standifer

Cover Design by: Scott Woods

A CIP record for this book is available from the Library of Congress Cataloging-in-Publication Data

BrickCaveBooks.com
2018

TABLE OF CONTENTS

PUBLISHER INFO

"10 Ways Kanye West is Not Prince" was a commissioned work courtesy of a bevy of funders through Kickstarter in August 2015.

"Every Prince Fan Is the World's Biggest Prince Fan" originally appeared on Legacy.com in April 2017.

ACKNOWLEDGEMENTS

No fan is so deep that they don't need a little help from their friends now and then for a project like this, and I needed plenty of help.

Special thanks for this edition must go to Erica Thompson, who listened to many of my rants and was there at the generation of many of the ideas that made their way into this book; KaNisa Williams, who hooked a brother up multiple times when I needed to get my ears or eyes on something that came up short in my own collection; PrinceVault.com for being the go-to resource for Prince minutiae; Rachel Kayla for being a comic book collecting fiend; and Paisley Park for opening the doors a little wider so fans could get in there and do the kind of processing that makes a book like this possible.

OTHER BRICK CAVE TITLES FROM SCOTT WOODS

 *We Over Here Now* (2013)

 *Urban Contemporary History Month* (2016)

 *Prince & Little Weird Black Boy Gods* (eBook Edition) (2017)

Prince & Little Weird Black Boy Gods
by Scott Woods

BRICK CAVE BOOKS
BrickCaveBooks.com

INTRODUCTION

We live in an age where everyone thinks people care what they think, an impression somehow both patently false and completely impenetrable at the same time. Nobody cares about what you post online until, one day, it seems everyone cares about what you post online. And just as soon as something you care about makes a splash, the next day you're likely back to levels of silence bordering on rude. A lot of people take these dips and crests in the interest market personally. Me, not so much. I generally write what I want and you either dig it or not, but I said what I said. Because of this admittedly spoiled brat platform, I tend to write almost exclusively about things I care about, and the more I care about them, the more times I revisit them and the more words those things get. Outside of my experience as a black person in America or poetry, it is unlikely that I've written about anything more than I have Prince Rogers Nelson.

I've read most books written about Prince and I can tell you that, with very few exceptions, most of them suck. This book will certainly suck to someone else, and mostly for the same reasons as most Prince books suck: it won't tell you anything about Prince that you didn't know. The difference with this book is that this isn't a book of rehashed Prince anecdotes passing itself off as a tell-all. This is a book of fan anecdotes attempting to unpack a relationship between a star and his fan.

Speaking at Prince's memorial service, musician/producer and Revolutionary Wendy Melvoin dropped the following nugget: "Being creative is how you can talk to him. If you're being creative, he will talk to you." That quote struck me. It wasn't so much that it contained a new concept as put words to the thing that I had kind of been doing every time I wrote something about Prince. Conversely, this book is a collection of conversations between Prince and I, some before he died, some after. Sometimes I was striving to say thank you, sometimes to admonish. Always I have been talking to my distant, really-bad-at-staying-in-touch friend. Now, just over a year after his death, I feel like I lost a friend I've known my whole life, and his music is how he spoke to me. I tried to speak back with my actions but if I'm completely honest, there is a part of me that feels guilt at not having worked hard enough with the life I've been given for him to have heard me. It is a real guilt. I took all of his gifts and he got none of mine because I didn't work hard enough. I feel like a bad friend. That's how important Prince is to me. And that's how important he is to a lot of people who didn't write thousands of words to prove it. Some of us danced. Some of us played our instruments harder. Some of us painted him onto the sides of buildings. All of us are, on some level, just trying to speak with our friend.

I hope you dig reading this as much as I dug going back through some of the stuff I've done over the years, as well as putting together some new or previously unshared material. Prince isn't the only one with a vault (though he's the only one with a real one. I just have stackable plastic storage boxes).

Scott Woods
General of the Purple Army
Columbus, Ohio Division
Class of 1979

ESSAYS

THINGS I AM REASONABLY SURE PRINCE HAS NEVER DONE
(2016)

1. Replaced toner in a copy machine
2. Manned the grill
3. Needed proof of ID
4. Played for exposure
5. Used a feather duster on a piece of furniture
6. Worked part time in a five and dime
7. Touched a black woman's hair unsolicited
8. Stayed on the phone with technical support
9. Used a coupon
10. Been the victim of identity theft
11. Pumped gas
12. Pledged frat
13. Filled out a job application
14. Eaten starfish
15. Made a lanyard at camp
16. Worn a 3X shirt
17. Worried about his credit rating
18. Fired a gun more than once
19. Thrown the first pitch
20. Used Coinstar
21. Cut grass
22. Kept change in the ashtray
23. Changed a lightbulb
24. Gone fishing
25. Shushed someone in a library
26. Cleaned a fish tank
27. Been put in handcuffs by anyone that wasn't a lover
28. Rode with a motorcycle gang
29. Used the word "synergy" in a business meeting
30. Stripped a bolt
31. Replied All by accident

32. Lost at spades
33. Put a "got next" token on a Galaga game
34. Sniffed milk to check its drinkability
35. Housesat
36. Pinched a finger because of tape measurer snapback
37. Worn a Thriller jacket
38. Compared a woman to a jeep
39. Played a game of Monopoly to completion
40. Failed a Rorschach test
41. Kicked a copy machine
42. Cashed soda bottles at a grocery store
43. Used a staple remover
44. Changed the oil in a car
45. Broke a heel in a sidewalk grate
46. Not smelled the roses
47. Gone caroling
48. Sang Rick James at karaoke
49. Consulted a road map
50. Killed a roach with a slipper
51. Testified before Congress
52. Changed a clock to Daylight Savings Time
53. Worn a tie to a job interview
54. Asked to use vacation time
55. Submitted work for peer review
56. Used left-handed scissors
57. Double flushed
58. Won a rap battle
59. Cleaned a gutter
60. Separated the stems on a Prince album cover
61. Shoveled a driveway
62. Read a romance novel
63. Eaten beans'n'weenies
64. Hit snooze
65. Rubbed Vicks Vaporub on his chest
66. Placed in a science fair

67. Spanked a child
68. Stood in line at the DMV
69. Stained a deck
70. Smoked wings
71. Wore a bike helmet
72. Used six months same as cash
73. Lost a thumbwrestling match
74. Upholstered a chair
75. Played Keno
76. Misapplied "their"
77. Been stung by a bee
78. Blown glass
79. Won at Scrabble
80. Cut Kool-Aid with liquor
81. Watched all of Cosmos
82. Used a Complete Idiot's Guide for anything
83. Run out of deodorant
84. Played marbles
85. Replaced a trashcan bag
86. Written a Yelp review
87. Made a pair of nunchakus out of a broom handle
88. Cut a toenail too close
89. Changed a diaper
90. Eaten a taco perfectly
91. Bet on red
92. Spent the night in anyone's guest room
93. Stood in line for the midnight sale of a GTA game
94. Hammered his thumb
95. Pledged a fraternity
96. Made a mixtape with other people's music on it
97. Taken a blown glass class
98. Hit a trifecta at the track
99. Tazed a bro
100. Grown old

PRINCE & LITTLE WEIRD BLACK BOY GODS
(2016)

(Written on April 22, 2016, the day after Prince died. - sew)

If you are, say, thirty-five years of age or older there is a 99% chance that you are no good right now. Not merely sad, but irreparably despondent. Verily, Shakespearean in your grief. Depending on how old or weird or gay or starstruck or black you were in 1984, *Purple Rain* was either an awakening, a testimony or an affirmation.

Current mood: I am hating anything that does not recognize this moment, that would dare advertise anything—ANYTHING—while this mourning is taking place. This is not just another stick on the pile of celebrity deaths. This is the end of a way of life, of a sound, of real genius. There are plenty of famous people left to love, even musical geniuses, but there is no one left who better epitomized what the Complete and Free Artistic Creative is capable of. Prince composed music in the way DaVinci unlocked the secrets of motion and the body and the universe. Prince was musically motion, body and universe; this funk drum plus that rock riff times this classical string quartet. There was nothing he could not do musically, nothing he could not create had he but the will. He was as close to Pan - in art, in gravitas, in appetite—as man will ever come.

Some of these emotions are not sentiments Prince would approve of, so in his honor I am trying to keep a lid on the emotional hyperbole, but it is difficult. Setting aside that there is almost nothing you can say about musical genius in the abstract that does not apply in the specific to Prince, I grew up with him in a way I did not grow up with other artists. Prince has been a presence in my life since I was a child, since I was able to discern what a record was for. Everybody liked Prince, though he represented different things to each interested party. Speaking from experience, what he represented to many little weird black boys was the strength inherent in a sensitive and self-knowing cool, particularly boys who knew more than they should at the ages they embodied by circumstance, nature, or both. I was a "both," a child acting out and acted upon, and at every turn Prince was there, breaking into my life with a lesson or challenge. Lost your girl?

Prince was there. Questioning your faith? Prince was there. Needed to unpack why your sensitivities made you a target? Prince was there and had packed a lunch. His music was not just a soundtrack to my existence; it was life skills coaching, and that kind of thing went on for the first twenty five years of my life beyond my record collection. I would do/want/need something and Prince would step in as consigliere, drop the appropriate tarot card, then spin off in a flush of purple smoke and distorted rim shots.

Prince reinvented himself so frequently and thoroughly that I discovered or re-discovered him at least four distinct times in my life:

– 1979, aka The Pre-Purple Genesis.

Prince was how I knew going through my oldest brother Tim's record collection was wrong. I had been told to stay out of Tim's room, but that was an edict from a brother, not a parent. Parents have to be negotiated with; brothers may be disobeyed. Rifling through his numerous rows of records, I distinctly remember the first time I saw a Prince record, 1979's *Prince*. The cover was typical 1970s fare—no shirt, straight pimp hair, no smiling. No big deal there: everybody on albums in the 70s was shirtless. Even the jazz artists were shirtless. Flipping to the back to ascertain what kind of music might be contained therein, I came to discover the magnitude of my crime. Prince was on a horse—a Pegasus to be exact—all fuzzy lens, hair in the wind, fantastically black...and naked. Only God knew what to make of that back cover, and that's how I knew it was wrong. The Ohio Players covers that littered my brother's collection were soft-porn naughty, but the back cover of Prince was salacious to me. The titles didn't help matters: "Sexy Dancer", "When We're Dancing Close and Slow", "Bambi." That album got played immediately in an attempt to crack the code of homeboy's agenda. Needless to say, I liked the record, but was too young to get all of the implications. The lyric sheet helped, and "Bambi" became a bit of a sexual clinic.

– On what was surely a Wednesday in 1982 my mother abandoned my baby brother and I at church one evening.

A weeknight drop-in at Brentnell Ave—I'm sorry: Church of Christ of the Apostolic Faith—was a rare occurrence. She worked multiple jobs so we were consummate latchkey kids. This, however, was a special occasion: a church-initiated talk about the evils of secular music. This awkward after-school special was delivered by my favorite Sunday School teacher, Brother Ragin, who, in his trademark soft-spoken but don't-play voice, showed us slide after slide of the album covers of popular music from the time and the symbology embedded in them that sought to abscond with our childhoods, far from the warm embrace of Jesus (who had exactly zero hit records in 1982). Outside of the slide for Iron Maiden's *The Number of the Beast* (which I knew was a softball even at that age), I will never forget Brother Ragin pointing out the numerous sexual and satanic references on the cover of *1999*. "Here," he pointed out with a white wand, "is the number 1999, which, when you turn it upside down (slide, image now upside down) is the number 666 with a penis in front of it. You can see the veins in it." I was never sold on the 666 part (and as it turns out, neither was Prince) but the D was real. Quite real. And obvious, quite obvious, upside down or not. It was some slick business. I was hip enough at that age that the speech had the unintended effect of making me seek it out. I hadn't owned the album at that point, but I did soon after. It wasn't about the veiny 1 specifically. It was about what the veiny 1 suggested might be behind it, inside it, underneath its odd crotch. As it turns out it was heralding one of the best albums of the twentieth century, and the most Prince album in his entire oeuvre, before or since.

– In 9th grade I dated a hardcore Prince fan.
She was the first girl I had met that was a hardcore fan of a celebrity, and her worship of him was so thorough I feared for my relationship. I besmirched the clearly gender-suspect posters of him plastered all over her bedroom. Her single-shoulder studded trenchcoat draped over a chair we screwed on, all of the albums posed cover out, her Princeoglyph-adorned learner's guitar judging our teenage curves...all of it made me suck my teeth at him, questioning his sexuality in an attempt to make myself look more macho. It didn't work. She was patient, but Prince insisted I was doing it all wrong, and he was right. And years later my post-college bedroom would have every Prince poster I could score out of my local record store circuit. It was a proud collection that I fear my mother's basement has long

had its way with.

– Same girlfriend.

We skipped school to go see *Under the Cherry Moon*. It was shoddy and ridiculous and hilarious and the music...my god, the music was unreal; some blend of art house and funk and symphonic eye-fucks. I loved it where I could not love myself. Leaving her house in the middle of the night a day or so later, she let me borrow her cassette copy of *Parade*. When she asked for it back weeks later I pretended to not know where it was. In truth, I played that tape to dust out of love and creative bewilderment. I was still trying to be a musician then and I couldn't figure out why the black café-ness of "Do U Lie?" worked, or how he'd come to the drumming decisions on "New Position," a song vacillating in rhythm decisions from gated arena snares to cafeteria cardboard thumb-boxing to steel-pan backbeat, all in two minutes and twenty seconds. The entire affair sounded like it came from some lost and forgotten era in music, where black people emigrated to Paris not to sell their art, but blend it, then elevate it, then transcend it; the whole exodus in one record. And, oh yeah, here's a 98 minute black and white video to go with it, you classless neophytes. And I die in the end, so all of this goes with me, cabbageheads.

–––

Of course it rained yesterday. Typical Prince.

I should have left work early. Coming back from lunch to discover news of Prince's death, a co-worker and friend touched my shoulder. "I'm sorry, man," he says, and he knows to mean it. Another staffer trumpets my sadness to the newbs who do not think my grief is real, who have not been working with me long enough to have Prince fall out of my mouth as a common proselytization. In the pantheon of my influences, Prince was Zeus, and poems sprung whole from my mouth when I called upon his sigils: an album, a biography, a memory of a Detroit crush set to "International Lover." I own every notable text on Prince, and what I do not own, I have likely consumed. There is no Prince song I have not heard that he has seen fit to release, and there are many I own which he has not. I have written essays—long, long essays—on Prince. I have written poems about Prince, after Prince, as Prince. I have created experiments to establish the code of his greatness. I have fucked people up over Prince. I have even fucked Prince up over Prince. I have heard "Purple Rain" played in a Mississippi juke joint by a teenage wunderkind of the blues, resting easy in the knowledge that Prince was officially, in that blackest of black-ass moments, going nowhere.

And yet, I need the strength of ignorance reserved for 2Pac fans who swear he is alive, even now. I need their middle fingers aimed at all common sense, their upturned lips at evidence and autopsy photos, their barbershop-loud anti-world denial cache striking back at all of the never-ending silence they swear by. I needed it to get me to the end of my work day, to the car, to the ride home. I feared the ride home. I cannot yet listen to his music. I can watch one or two of the videos because I already know what's in all of them and can gauge what I can bear. But I cannot really talk about him yet, not well, not without it turning into The Only Thing That Needs To Happen In That Moment. I threw myself into work yesterday because library books don't speak and the children I often help do not know Prince. I am too curt, too short with anyone who might know who Prince was in any real way. He is not small talk to me, not yet. I should have left work because people who do know me and know what his passing means to me know where to find me and I am not ready for their condolences. I have not accepted it the way you accept a death. I bear the face of rebuke, I can feel it. I am not ready to bookend that magical and phenomenal career. I refuse to allow *HITnRUN Phase Two* to be the last Prince record released under his supervision. My heart cannot take it. I want to scream at his legal team to ease up for a day and let us have our illegal mourning, just for one day.

I did not have the musical well or will to absorb Prince's lessons on the level of a musician. Some of those lessons I applied to the music I was able to create, but ultimately Prince would bond with the DNA of my life at large, like he did for most of us. For those of us who were not musicians, he would inform our grind: our sense of fashion or how we kissed our lovers or every crowd "Whooo" when you heard him peel his hand down the length of a piano at the beginning of "Do Me Baby." There always seemed to be a crowd "whoooing," even if it was in your car, alone, on your way to anywhere. I can't listen to his music yet, but I know these things will always be true of it.

In the late 1980s *Ebony* magazine published an article that was kind of a lark, a "Where will these black celebrities be in 50 years?" or some such thing. They had Jesse Jackson and Eddie Murphy as president and VP respectively, captured in a *New Yorker* style rendering of them in front of the White House, that sort of thing. One section of the satire suggested that Prince would be playing in a small Las Vegas lounge, fat and trying to relive his glory days between bar tabs. I'd give no small amount of precious things to make that the end of the story.

Dave Chappelle's "True Hollywood Stories with Charlie Murphy" skit about a basketball-playing Prince is classic television because it is stop-breathing funny. It is also one of those rare instances in which we get a glimpse into the mysterious world of Prince as a person, and it leaves us with more questions than answers. If you're a longtime fan you already heard from someone somewhere that he played ball, and not just in high school. But to have it told to us as a genuine experience was almost more than a Prince stan's heart could stand. Coming up, you took your Prince scraps where you could get them. There was no internet lying in wait behind every rock and turn, every cellphone a body cam, TMZ skull-fucking every corpse before it cooled. Prince was the last real pop enigma. No one cares about anyone else's mystery, and if your mystery isn't turning out art like *Sign O' the Times*, who cares what you're hiding? Go live your lives, false idols. I'm still trying to figure out what elixir Prince drank that made "Something in the Water (Does Not Compute)" fall out of his head. How he stayed out of the mix of this world we have made—aspects of which he ushered in but more or less refused to partake of when they became common and base and knowable—I'll never know. In a world where a celebrity can't hide how much they tip in a restaurant without the amount becoming an international headline, Prince remained above it all. We thought he was hiding, but one look at his output—his recordings, his vault, the quality of his live shows, the stories—shows us that he wasn't hiding so much as he always had better things to do, that there was always more to apply one's self to.

– – –

I have tried to ascertain why I care, beyond the music. Why my stomach churns at the notion of logging onto the internet and having people post rampantly and randomly about someone that, while I could teach classes about him, I did not know, was never going to know. What was Prince to me, exactly? I don't cry over celebrities, ever. Why did I cry at work? Why did I need to lock myself into a bathroom and grieve with real tears? He was too young to see as a father figure, too distant to see as cousin, too Prince to be a brother. The closest relationship I can ascribe to us is friend. I have lost my friend. Like all strong and real friendships, he was there when I needed a little help, and occasionally I took him to task, often relentless in my admonishments of his creative decisions or a weak album. It was all love, a real I-want-the-best-for-you love. Even his weak albums contained more pure musicianship than almost every record released alongside it in any given year. Even if I did not like the destinations, the rides were generally worth the price of the ticket. Even when I hated a record, I knew what it took to make it, my long-suffering faith making me stand frenzied on its neck, screaming, "You can't write 'The Beautiful Ones' and then come back with this!"

This is not a think piece or an article or an assignment or click bait. This is a eulogy. My friend died yesterday. You can't tell me shit about my friend or this moment. The autopsy will say whatever it has to say. For myself, I must reconcile a world wherein what few idols I bother claiming are stepping down from the dais I have erected, that I am losing my religion, and that the largest and central throne on the Mount Olympus of my influences now sits vacant. I must come to terms with a world in which there is no Prince, that what we have is all that we will ever have, that purple is just going to be a color again. All pantheons pass.

See you on the other side, Prince. I promise not to bring any demos or make any pancake jokes. I cannot promise that I will not bring a basketball. Some things, cousin, you just have to see for yourself.

THE DAY I DISCOVERED *PRINCE* (BY WAY OF REVIEW)
(2017)

I have mentioned on multiple occasions that I recall very distinctly the day that I discovered *Prince*. Depending on the point of a given article or essay, I've cherry-picked which aspects of the story to bring to the fore, but considering the amount of words I've spent on Prince over the years it seems only fair to make an official account of how it all began. To this end I will attempt to recreate that fateful day in 1979 here, the details as close to reality as my fallible memory allows.

Side one
1. "I Wanna Be Your Lover"
This song sucked me in because I knew this song. It had been on the radio and I recognized it immediately. I had just never pieced together that the naked man on the cover of the otherwise boring record wrote that cool song.

2. "Why You Wanna Treat Me So Bad?"
Now this was a sentiment I could relate to. While laboring under no pretense that folks were going 'round town talking about me, by this point in my life I had broken up with at least three girls. (Well, maybe 2.5. I am not convinced Melissa knew we were supposed to be in a relationship, but we had shared the smell of each other's bellybutton fingers in class, so we had a history.)

3. "Sexy Dancer"
I knew what sexy meant and found things sexy: ponytails, playground kisses, HBO after 10 PM. And I knew dancing because I was a music-loving child. I even knew what sexy dancing was because I watched Soul Train every week. The Soul Train line was the single sexiest thing on television in the 70s if you didn't subscribe to HBO or have brothers who kept porn under their beds (I did not). So while I wasn't sure what "creaming" was, I knew what wanting someone's body meant.

4. "When We're Dancing Close and Slow"

I did not practice slow dancing to this by myself the first time I listened to this song, but it did eventually happen. The sentiment of the first half of the song was innocent enough, and the groove was perfect for basement slow dancing I was never going to do, as it turned out. But the nasty parts? I locked those away in my nappy head for reasons unknown to me at the time, but that would become crystal clear years later, when dancing was not the goal of putting this song on.

(Here I'd like to point out that I had to flip over a physical vinyl record to continue my journey. At this point it was a choice, but also, at this point I was invested. I flipped the record and kept the party going.)

Side two
5. "With You"

After the salacious and funky nature of the first side I was lulled into an almost pastoral sense of comfort by "With You." It was old school sweet, a song so sentimental it bordered on naïve. Except for the throwaway bit about laying with someone, the rest of the stuff on here was perfectly placed for an already morose and longing-addled romantic. And the way he held and rose his voice at the end was kind of mind-blowing.

6. "Bambi"

...and then this happened. This is the song that changed everything. All of a sudden I wasn't dancing slow or sexy, wasn't on a romantic or black album at all. With the opening electric guitar riffs ripping into the air I had suddenly been catapulted back upstairs into other older brother Stephen's room, the brother who listened to all of the white rock music my brother Tim didn't. I could scarcely believe this was the same musician. And then he started singing. Now, I was hip to what sex was as a concept, but I knew nothing about bisexuality. And even if I had heard of it at this point, it was still 1979. Even if I hadn't been a child at the time I still very likely would have had aggressively non-progressive views on the matter. As it turns out, by the end of the song I found the idea of women-on-women sex intriguing, and completely beyond my ability to picture. And if I'm completely honest, when Prince sang "I'm gonna show you what it's like to be loved by a man," I didn't know what it was a man was supposed to really be doing that was so instructive, or what he was trying to fix. Ultimately, I was mostly befuddled by this song and had discovered the first of what would be many Prince mysteries.

7. "Still Waiting"

Another mostly saccharine offering whose doo-wop sensibilities wouldn't have appealed to me even if they hadn't come on the heels of just having learned that bisexuality was real and could be cured by the really earnest penis of an effeminate sounding man who rode mythological creatures in the nude.

8. "I Feel for You"

I liked this just fine before Chaka Khan would have her way with it five years later. It was funky and playful—like me—and I could totally get on board with Prince's analysis of the situation at that age: I have a feeling when I'm around you. It is warm. It is mainly a physical thing. There is no place I'd rather be. I think I'm in love. I mean, that was basically my interaction with every girl until I was ten. I'm pretty sure I wrote each of those lines at some point before fourth grade and gave them to a girl. Also, for you trivia buffs out there, it's worth noting that Chaka's version of this song represents the only time someone has covered a Prince song better than Prince.

9. "It's Gonna Be Lonely"

He tried to warn me, but I wouldn't listen. I came back to this song over and over again at the end of innumerable break-ups as I grew up, and all I had to show for it was a lot of bad poetry and dozens of misspent hours imagining that girls who had broken up with me might be playing this song at the same time I was. Alas.

10 WAYS KANYE WEST IS NOT PRINCE
(2015)

(This essay began as a dare. Without repeating too much of what is already in the essay, in August of 2015, I had posted something along the lines of "Yeah, L.A. Reid's statement is ridiculous, and I can prove it empirically, but no way I'm doing that for free. Pay me $100 and I'll do it." I raised $150. It's been slightly edited since I couldn't include the graphs and pics.—sew)

> *Go show your slaves how choleric you are*
> *And make your bondmen tremble. Must I budge?*
> *Must I observe you? Must I stand and crouch*
> *Under your testy humor? By the gods,*
> *You shall digest the venom of your spleen,*
> *Though it do split you. For from this day forth,*
> *I'll use you for my mirth, yea, for my laughter,*
> *When you are waspish.*

– Brutus, Julius Caesar, Act 4, Scene 3.

I need to make clear what is not happening here: I am not here to kick Kanye West in the nuts for twenty pages. I'm not here to tell you that West is not an artist or that you shouldn't buy his records or listen to his music or buy his shoes. How people culturally navigate Kanye West doesn't affect a single facet of my life. This is not a hit piece, though admittedly such pieces wouldn't admit it if they were. Understanding how this essay might be perceived, all I can do is tell you what I did or did not set out to do. So no, I am not here to labor over the many ways in which I despise Kanye West. There will be instances during the course of this bushwhacking where this will not seem to be the case, not by a long shot. I assure you that the intention of such moments is not gross flippancy or injected merely for effect. I maintain that such moments have but one true ambition: to illustrate and support the main thesis. I do not like most of West's art—almost nothing after the first half of Graduation—nor do I think I would like him as a person. But these are merely infusions, bits of vegetables simmering in the roux of my larger case. They're flavoring, but nothing that makes the meal any less what you ordered.

HOW WE GOT HERE

Back in 2011 notable R&B producer, record label exec and ripper-offer of TLC L.A. Reid stated that, in his esteemed opinion, Kanye West was "one of the greatest if not the greatest performers, entertainers, musicians of all time." By itself, this statement hardly bears noting. It's one of countless examples of insider back-patting one commits despite any relationship to reality in an attempt to remain relevant to whatever demographic still spends actual money on records instead of bootlegging it like the rest of the world. I get it. Stay cool, L.A. Reid.

But when he went on to say:

"People may not recognize it today, but I promise you a few years from today we're going to look back and say, 'Oh my God, what an amazing, amazing talent.' People love Kanye for sure, but he's great, great. I mean on the level of Prince. But modern day, he's hip-hop. He's not the same thing. He doesn't play guitar, he doesn't play piano. He's not that kind of performer, but for hip-hop he is a king."

…I could countenance no more.

As a die-hard life-long Prince fan, this slap in the face would be ridiculous if it were happening in my barbershop, let alone on a national media platform like BET. Like, flip-a-table-full-of-newborn-babies ridiculous. But when it comes from someone who runs a record label, whose job it is to act as a gatekeeper to what music millions of people might possibly encounter? Well, that's practically an actionable offense. The problem in that moment was that this act concerns parties I find so artistically reprehensible that I fear my hands may combust into flame while writing about them, which is how I navigate these glitches in the cultural matrix: I write them into the ground.

But it's L. A. Reid. What person living in 2015 cares what L.A. Reid thinks about anything? The only part of his interview BET saw fit to highlight was the part about someone else's career that he had nothing to do with.

Key ❢ Still, people are lazy, and lazy people can still change history. We read headlines and then write responses to them longer than the articles. We take these kinds of bon mots and we run with them. And sometimes in our running we create enough friction to make an icon out of something that had no business making its way off of YouTube. Enough communal will can make something become newsworthy, which arguably makes it important, which places it in a position to make it iconic…which, when left unchecked, can accidentally be labeled "influential" and "great," paying little mind to what that influence has wrought, what qualifiers might suit it, or if that greatness is legitimate. If people want to believe that Kanye West is great, I can more or less live with that. It's their poster and they can put it on whatever bedroom wall they want so long as it isn't mine. What I cannot abide is attempting to fashion someone's greatness by comparing them to Prince and that person be Kanye West. Kanye West may very well be talented and engaging his art form at a better than average or even skillful level. But there are a lot of artists you can compare him to that don't make you sound like a tool before you get to Prince levels of greatness. And I simply won't have it. ❂

This investigation isn't so much about listing the differences between the two artists—you don't have the bandwidth and I don't have the long-term finger strength for that exercise—as it is about combating attempts to re-define greatness in a negative direction. Because let's be honest: Kanye West and Prince couldn't be more dissimilar, and those differences are largely apparent to even the most musically illiterate among us. So there is a caprice at work here. That said, greatness as a concept is subjective, but is less subjective than, say, if I like a particular song or not. There are qualitative and quantitative elements to greatness that go beyond whether or not something is good. Lots of things that are great aren't actually good or healthy or wise. Under that logic, one can argue that West remains great no matter what comparison someone might arbitrarily make on his behalf.

At the same time it's important to bear in mind that there is very little empirical evidence that can be applied to discussions like this, and that for all of the centuries of art criticism that exists, none of it has ever yielded a dissection that wasn't, at its base, subjective. Democratic, perhaps, but not objective. At the end of 50 years of *Rolling Stone*, 80 years of *DownBeat*, 27 years of *The Source*, 60 years of the *Village Voice*, and 90 years of *The New Yorker*, no such method has ever been devised. And yet, great art exists. Great artists persist. We erect monuments and install holidays in light of their greatness. Greatness exists. It has a cause and an effect, and it forms as a residual function of cultural and social capital bestowed by the people. Greatness, while contestable, is real.

Sway might not have had the answers, but I do.

WHY BOTHER?

Arguably the only people who think Kanye West is the greatest artist of this or any other generation are either dense fanatics, hyperbolic media writers, Kanye West himself, or are people who were shaken at a very young age by an extremely powerful nanny. So why bother? It's a rude if valid question to which I have three answers: two equally rude-but-still-true ones, and a congenial-but-longer one.

1. Because I was paid to.
2. Because knowing something is true doesn't mean it isn't worth investigating further. We know other planets exist. Should we not benefit from all of the things investigating those planets might yield in science, medicine, education, culture, and philosophy?
3. Because Stephanie Mills can't be the only real motherfucker in the greatness game.

Before MTV finally broke down and started playing videos by black artists, BET ran a video/interview show called *Video Soul*, hosted for years by the eternally affable Donnie Simpson, who seemingly never interviewed an artist he didn't like. He was the Walter Cronkite of black music journalism, as Video Soul was the CNN of black music. Simpson was a champion of black mainstream music, and the 80s was a great time to be such a champion: rap was starting to break out of the streets and into the American consciousness, Michael Jackson was still a Michael Jackson you could respect, BET hadn't gone full ratchet yet, and you still had to be able to sing to get a record deal. For nearly the length of a generation Video Soul broke emerging and returning black acts to new and larger audiences, and some artists never had a better interview than one they got from Donnie Simpson.

Basically, *Video Soul* was the shit.

One afternoon, around 1989, R&B legend Stephanie Mills sat on the couch across from Simpson, pleasant and beautiful as you please. Simpson asked her about the comparison that many people had been making between the iconic Luther Vandross (who was still at the height of his powers at the time) and notably gifted newcomer David Peaston, who was riding pretty high on the charts with the single "Two Wrongs (Don't Make It Right)." Mills chuckled and said something like, "Oh, no. He's no Luther. I can see why some people might say that, because of his weight or something, but that's about where the similarities end. But no, not Luther." I don't know who did what after that—who called who, who sent whom a copy of the interview, or how Peaston felt about the comparison or Mills's course correction. I imagine the comparisons were flattering and the public correction was gut-wrenching. I can tell you this much for sure: you never heard anyone comparing Peaston to Vandross again.

There are just some things you don't compare, certain things you just don't say.

So look: don't blame me for writing this. Blame L.A. Reid for saying it. Blame BET for highlighting it. Blame the internet for allowing this suggestion to tattoo itself across its underbelly of free-wheeling ignorance. I was perfectly content to write my poems and books and be fair-to-middling awesome. If you were getting along just fine in your life without dealing with this question, you'll likely survive not reading this essay, as well. My world, however, could not brook such tragedy. Any comparisons to Prince in this arena are worth at least a cursory mental exercise where I'm from. Trying to compare someone like Kanye West to Prince on the matter of greatness literally sets off a red-belled alarm in my house that can only be quelled by repeat listens of *Sign O' The Times* until the voices stop or a full-bore investigation. Obviously, my copy of *Sign O' The Times* is on loan.

10 WAYS KANYE WEST IS NOT PRINCE

1) Prince is more talented.

People have been attempting to quantify talent since a caveman's buddy was underwhelmed by his hand painting of the big hunt that day. People have always felt the need to crown someone over another in every era of every culture. How we arrive at these decisions used to be simple: this gladiator survived the pit. This musician played harpsichord with incredible intricacy. This jet pilot made it out of the danger zone. Even in situations in which ignorance of all the possible candidates for reward in a particular field (think of all the awesome musicians sans record deal) allows us to bypass whole swathes of contributors to enthrone a select few, cream has a way of rising to the top in most situations. We might argue about who deserves the top spot in a field, but generally speaking the person who holds the top spot in a field is still an extremely talented individual. Yet, with the intersection of slavish machine-wrought hype and calculating management, culture imbalances in quality/reward occur. At some point one could bully their way into honor.

Fortunately we're not faced with such a dilemma here: Prince can sing, dance, compose, play, produce, engineer, act, envision, and execute said vision better than Kanye West. Within each of those line item talents Prince outstrips West by a Minneapolis winter mile.

In the first two categories, there is no debate. Kanye can't sing, period, ever. Even with the aid (or masquerade) of auto-tune, *808s and Heartbreaks* still sounds more earnest than artistic, and "earnest" is a strong word to use about a record on which the artist hides his inability to convey melodic content with intentionally incorrect electronic masking. If we are brutally honest, many people cut this record a lot of slack because they know that he was hurting as a person after the death of his mother rather than because of any genuinely compelling art contained therein. What was largely being heralded as a new direction for music was mostly just a new direction for Kanye, and for his fans they are largely one in the same. Just know that somewhere, Roger Troutman is dropping a digital tear every time someone uses auto-tune, not because he would not approve, but because you can still hear "More Bounce to the Ounce" in any black club or skating rink if you stay long enough and people keep calling 808s a "game changer."

As regards dancing, I don't care about dancing in general, but I'm trying to be thorough here. Just know that this is also a wash for West. Kanye can bounce, but he cannot dance. No one in the history of music reviews has ever remarked at how much more captivating West's art became once he put one foot in front of the other. By contrast, Prince is an amazing dancer,

Talent Comparison

	Prince	KANYE WEST
Singing	✓	
Dancing	✓	
Songwriting	✓	
Musicianship	✓	
Production	✓	
Engineering	✓	
Acting	✓	
Vision	✓	
Execution of vision	✓	

fig. 1

despite no one knowing what he was doing to those speakers in *Purple Rain* for the length of "Darling Nikki." The splits, the twirls, the heels, the half nudity...all in service to entertaining you with his body while his mouth was taking a break.

Songwriting could go either way depending on what you like until you consider that Prince has written songs that will remain in the lexicon of American music for a hundred years after he's gone, composed largely on instruments that anyone can learn to play, which perpetuates the resonance of his compositional skill. 90% of Kanye's music is largely fashioned as an electronic construct that requires a record player set to 45 rpm. For similar reasons, Prince's ability to play multiple instruments at an expert level—which he has been doing professionally since he was eighteen—destroys anything resembling musicianship from Kanye, which as near as anyone can tell largely consists of filing through a record crate and speeding up Chaka Khan vocals ("Through the Fire"). Even L.A. Reid notes in his grand pronouncement that Kanye doesn't play any instruments, which should have made him retract his entire statement before I ever saw it, but whatever.

Prince developed new ways to manipulate production values and, on occasion, instruments themselves. Prince frequently manipulated drum machines and synthesizers to suit his ideas, introducing signature sounds, branding his music as unique and modern. Kanye, eh, less so, and certainly nothing groundbreaking. He's not even the best person to utilize chipmunk breaks, let alone from-metronome-scratch musical production values. West produced hits, but West didn't do so in a vacuum or alone.

While we can find much to laugh about in Prince's acting resume (*Purple Rain* was serviceable, but everything after that is, admittedly, comic fodder for the most part), his attempts to engage audiences cinematically outstrip Kanye's many attempts to resell himself to us as himself in little more than long music videos, with the rare instance of stepping outside of himself to cameo as an MTV veejay in *Anchorman 2*. Despite the argument that Prince, too, largely plays versions of himself in films (and exactly himself in an episode of *New Girl*), I think we can all agree that Prince as a persona is far more interesting than Kanye as a persona, and not just because Prince is fiercely private. It's because Prince isn't an instantly grating personality or prone to tantrums around other grown folks.

I'll speak more to vision below, but know that it's coming. Rest assured, Prince has that on lock. For now, I'll leave you with this nugget of Kanye wisdom:

"Taylor Swift beat Beyoncé at the Grammys? Beyoncé be dancing in heels and shit."

Yeah. Hey, you know who else be dancing in heels and shit? Prince. Sometimes while he's playing a guitar one-handed or jumping off of a piano.

2) Prince is more prolific.

For most people, Prince would win this fight by virtue of having a record contract since he was eighteen...when West was a year old. Volume metrics go a long way in the music business. By the time West debuted *College Dropout* in 2004, Prince had already released 26 albums, scored 6 movies, and been on 20 tours. In the year that *College Dropout* dropped, Prince released three albums (*Musicology, The Chocolate Invasion,* and *The Slaughterhouse*) and was mounting what was arguably his fifth comeback. As of this writing Prince has released 32 studio albums, and at least 6 of them were multiple discs. Since 2004 West has released 7 albums in 9

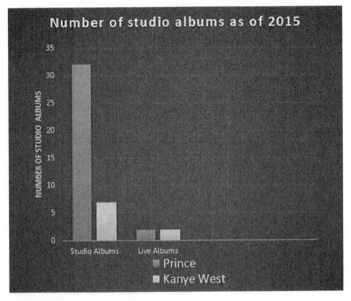

fig. 2

years. In the same amount of time, Prince has also released 7 albums, 2 of them at the same time in 2014. And none of Prince's albums were co-chaired by Jay-Z.

I will be the first to admit that a straight disc count is not a solid gauge of greatness. This is at least true because it's unfair in a time/space fashion, but also because a discography of Prince releases is only a fractional indication of how prolific Prince is. Prince has so much music he can't release it all (one of the sticking points he had with Warner Brothers for years: they wanted to keep him to a manageable one album per year and he wanted to be the internet twenty years before it was real). Prince has so much music that it is in danger of decaying before it can ever be heard. Prince has songs that have never seen the light of day that are more famous—and better—than albums he has released. By contrast, Kanye less than ten albums, and a handful of mixtapes that largely don't advance his stock. Kanye doesn't have a ton of unreleased material that people are clamoring for. Kanye simply doesn't have enough songs to win this fight any way you fight it.

But let's say you're really adamant about not comparing pound-for-pound output because it's too skewed against Kanye on the basis of when he was born. Fine: here are two ways to level the field and (spoiler alert) Prince still wins both arguments:

Method 1) Top number of albums vs. top number of albums.

As of this writing West has six solo studio albums to his name. Let us pretend that they are all good records. If we kept Prince down to his best six albums, Kanye loses that all day, every day. For the record, here are the best six Prince albums (in no order):

Purple Rain
Sign O' the Times
1999
Controversy
Dirty Mind
Parade

Again, no contest. Any one of these records is better than every album Kanye West has produced. Setting all of them together next to Kanye's entire oeuvre is tantamount to a hate crime.

Method 2) Comparative career window output.

We could try to compare relative career windows based on time, holding Prince down to any ten year period compared to Kanye's entire ten year career (2004—2013). Here's what that looks like:

If we go from 1978 (Prince's debut, *For You*) through 1987 (*Sign O' the Times*), not only does Kanye have to contend with *Times*, but he still has to measure up against *1999*, *Controversy* and *Purple Rain*...basically Prince in his prime. No contest.

If we go 1985 (just after *Purple Rain*, to show mercy) through 1994 (*Come* and *The Black Album*) we're still talking about *Sign O' the Times*, *Parade* and the *Batman* soundtrack. No contest.

If we go from 2004 (when Kanye came out) through 2015 you really only have to contend with *Musicology* and *Prince* about 13 years past his prime, but understand that we have to discount 25 previous years of work and already in-stone greatness to even give Kanye a fighting chance.

So for this to even resemble a contest I have to wreck Prince's entire career just to get Kanye to the table so he can attempt to beat Prince's scraps (*3121*, *Planet Earth*, etc.).

"Congratulations," I guess?

3) Prince is more influential.

When you speak about Prince's influence on other artists, the range is wide, the road long, and the vein runs deep. There are artists who have committed their entire careers to sounding like some version of Prince (D'Angelo, Ready for the World, Ginuwine, etc.), and Prince has whole eras that one can choose as a lane: Purple Prince, French Prince, Garage Prince, Nasty Prince, Religious Prince, Jazz Prince, Techno Prince, Black Prince, White Prince, Guitar Prince. Some artists just borrow parts (Janelle Monae, Miguel, Marsha Ambrosius, everybody who released an R&B record between 1985 and 1995), some just steal (Alecia Keys). His music has inspired acts in almost every genre of music. When we speak of him we say his name in the same breath as other uncontestable greats: Stevie Wonder, Marvin Gaye, Whitney Houston, Luther Vandross, Donny Hathaway, Michael Jackson, James Brown...all game-changing artists, that game being putting out incredible song after incredible song over a long period of time. Prince is one of the reasons why we have parental advisory stickers on albums. Prince spawned numerous side acts, some of whom went on to become icons in their own right. Prince was single-handedly responsible for trifling R&B as we know it, opening the door to the Champagne Room for acts like R. Kelly, Jodeci and their ilk. Prince has been name checked as an influence by artists like D'Angelo, Jill Scott, Terence Trent D'Arby, and countless others. His professional nemesis was Michael Jackson, who remains arguably the greatest live musical entertainer of all time.

Kanye West has influenced acts like Drake, Plies, Chance, and a half-generation of rappers that no one in the industry wouldn't debate is a degraded field at best. When Prince was at his peak, he was arguably one of the world's best singers performing the best popular songs played with the best technique. Even a basic Kanye discussion comes with so many qualifiers—"He's a rap genius" or "He's going to make (obscure genre) mainstream" or "He's just an average rapper but he's a great producer"—I'm not sure why people waste their time attempting to convince anyone of his so-called greatness.

4) Prince had to do more with less against more.

I understand why people think Kanye is great. Seriously, I get it: if you came up on Kanye's music—meaning you were born after, say, 1992 and were twelve when *College Dropout* was released and can actually stomach mainstream music today for longer than five minutes—he's your version of Michael Jackson and Prince. Trust me when I say I understand your fanaticism. We used to go nuts over MJ and Prince. They were our Beatles in 1984. People were sewing zippers onto leather jackets trying to look like MJ, and *Purple Rain* gave birth to more jheri curls than *Ebony* magazine. I know what it's like to live under an icon several times over, especially one with the ability to suck up media bandwidth with the kind of gravity West is capable of generating.

But let's be clear: Prince used to do that with a song you didn't want your parents to hear ("Head"), or by writing a whole album of songs you didn't want your parents to hear (*Dirty Mind, 1999*), and he had to do it when you actually had to exhibit some degree of musical talent to participate in the industry. Prince was trying to sell records alongside Lionel Ritchie (who still sold more albums in 2012 than every rapper you can name 29 years after "Hello") and DeBarge (which was like a whole family of Princes) and Stevie Wonder (80s Wonder, but still able to knock a hit out the park when he needed to). And, oh yeah, *Thriller*, which every corner of the industry was still reeling from a year after the fact. And these were just the acts he was vying for attention over in 1984. And those were just a handful of hit-makers; he still had to contend with definitive (and in some cases, legendary) albums from Cameo (*She's Strange*), Tina Turner (*Private Dancer*), Sade (*Diamond Life*), Billy Ocean (*Suddenly*), Jermaine Jackson (*Jermaine Jackson*) and his whole damned family (*Victory*), New Edition (*New Edition*), and more. And those were just the black acts, which has rarely been Prince's only wheelhouse. And if that weren't enough, Prince was in heavy competition with himself that year: he wrote most of the music for both The Time's *Ice Cream Castle* and Sheila E.'s *The Glamorous Life*, not to mention going up against Chaka Khan's biggest hit ever, a cover of his "I Feel For You."

I don't care how you feel about Kanye West: you have to admit that's a hell of a field.

Of course, it's a different world, by which I mean it has different social and cultural rhythms. Everything is faster now, and media expectations are different. Music is, for all intents and purposes, free, owned largely by choice, not necessity. Album release dates are a joke, and have been long before Beyonce cold-cocked everyone's annual "Best of the Year" charts in 2013. And all of this swirls underneath the one observation that we're all too scared to say out loud: music just sucks some years.

Which brings us squarely to the rap question.

Hip-hop as a commercial art is worse now than it was ten years ago, and ten years ago it was struggling. While such statements are traditionally pigeon-holed as being generational arguments of taste, I don't know anyone who would suggest with a straight face that even half of the rappers on a Billboard chart would stack up artistically against even a middle of the field rapper from 1995. Three of the top ten songs on Billboard's rap chart for August 8, 2015 are from Fetty Wap.

A Meek Mill versus Drake pillow fight is what's passing for rap beef in 2015. That's a long drop from Jay-Z vs. Nas or Lil Kim vs. Foxy Brown. That's arguably a long drop from Ice T vs. Soulja Boy, which was a battle between two highly suspect rappers, but was symbolic of so much more about hip-hop than who was a garbage rapper. And it's not just a matter of taste: find anyone willing to go on record that mainstream hip-hop isn't simpler, dumber, and less diverse in tone and scope than it was just ten years ago. And while it is easy to say "Mainstream rap always sucked," that's not true: Biggie and 2Pac were the mainstream. NWA and Public Enemy occupied the mainstream. Wu-Tang Clan lorded over the mainstream as a series of franchise units. And while it is easy to point out that good rappers still exist, that's not largely true of the art in the mainstream now, and even the examples of genuinely talented artists tend to age poorly once the check is cashed and the shine has worn off. Jay-Z and Kanye's *Watch the Throne* should have been the best rap record of 2011. It wasn't. It was just the most hyped. It probably had the most producers of any rap album in history, but it wasn't better musically or lyrically than Phonte's *Charity Starts At Home* or Pharoahe Monch's *W.A.R.* or a handful of others. That shouldn't have been true in any world, but such is the state of hip-hop: when you get to the top now you throw money and hype and names at your art where you used to throw your hunger. We used to be able to see qualitative diversity in the mainstream as well as the underground. What passes for a good rapper now didn't used to even make a b-side fifteen years ago. Instead, the radio feels like a flea market of bad ideas and broken sex toys that keeps telling my woman to take off her clothes and the internet is a vast and swelling tide of distractions that have nothing to do with music, for which West's career seems a perfect avatar.

West owes no small part of his success to the fact that he is participating in the music genre with the easiest on-ramp ever created by musicians. Regardless of how well West executes his art, rap wasn't that hard to do at the point during which he entered the game. If West were trying to break into 1999 rap he would have looked like a clown sitting on the shelves next to A *Prince Among Thieves* or *Things Fall Apart* or *I Am . . .* or *Black on Both Sides*. Now? The average rapper with a record deal is largely forgettable and the game has been that way for a long time.

5) Prince is more respected.

You get a sense of this truism in Reid's original statement, wherein he seeks to quantify West's greatness by comparing it to an inarguable greatness: Prince. At this point I hardly need to make a case for the amount of respect Prince has amassed in 40 years of grinding a high heeled boot in popular music's face.

What we can do is be honest about why Kanye fails on this count, and here's why: Kanye can't get respect for his art or his vision because his art is never allowed to stand on its own merits before he undermines it by saying something ridiculous. His vision never gets a chance to pan out.

Kanye tries to convince people that his art is great, not by rolling out progressive music with mind-blowing visual art to accompany it, but by talking about how great he is for having an idea or selling a lot of records to college kids. There is almost nothing West will not say or do to convince an audience of his art's power, except let the art speak for itself. How such vision is executed is part of what makes someone great and his music almost never gets a chance to prove itself because he can't stop telling us how he's Shakespeare and God wrapped up in a garbage bag tunic and shitty moon boots. Ultimately, of course, the music needs that kind of hype bump to get it to perform at the financial and cultural levels West needs to maintain his tastemaker façade, but on its own it is middle of the field arena rap at best.

Not to mention that it's a lot to ask of people to hand over respect to someone who maintains so little of it for audiences and other artists. He has nearly interrupted more award show acceptance speeches than Prince has given, and these will be the frames of choice in the highlight reel of his career; not his music, not his concerts, not his fashion. Being an uncontestable "jackass," to use the words of the President of the United States of America.

And by the way: when a sitting president calls you—on video—a "jackass" in the middle of waging two ground wars, massaging big banks' backs during a failed economy, launching tons of secret drone strikes, and maintaining an intensely unpopular invasion of citizens' privacies, you are so a jackass. Technically, Kanye could have responded with "Barack Obama doesn't care about black people" and we, as a people of the republic, would have had to stop and think about that one for a second. As it turns out, West is just a jackass.

…who, contrary to his own statements, doesn't respect artistry. The irony of West, who can't compose a song with fewer than three guest writers now, interrupting an awards speech by Beck, who believes so strongly in the music coming out of himself that he released a book of sheet music for songs he never recorded or released. Beck, who was smashing rap and rock on *Odelay* ten years before *College Dropout*. Kanye West wanted to school the world on the value of true artistry at Beck's expense. BECK. Remixing-Philip-Glass Beck. One-day-album-cover-project Beck. Visionary Beck. If it's any consolation, at the rate West is going his legacy won't be the music he leaves behind at all. It will be how many times he held our attention with a ridiculous statement or behavior (which, for the record, is hitting at an incident/album ratio of about 20:1 in favor of "I am the number one human being in music.")

What Prince must have been thinking, standing there, watching the not-so-new hotness try to make a point against pure musicianship by playing a petulant child at Beck's expense instead of making great music. Because when Prince wants to make a statement, that's how he does it: he releases a song about an issue or he sets up a community concert in Baltimore. He decides people could use an education on funk so he writes *Musicology*, then pimps the industry that spent years pimping him until they have to change the rules to stop him. He doesn't step into someone else's moment on stage while the world is watching. It would never occur to him to do so. When you're great, you don't have to dump on someone's moment to make a point. When you are capable of generating real, long-lasting content to engage people's taste, you don't have to play your own tastemaker to drive the point home.

When you have to tell people to respect you, they never will.

6) When Prince deigns to cover a song, it's covered.

"My greatest pain in life is that I will never be able to see myself perform live."
– Kanye West, 2009.

My greatest pain in life was watching Kanye West "perform" "Bohemian Rhapsody."

Queen's "Bohemian Rhapsody" is one of the greatest rock songs ever. I only say "one of" so as not to derail proof of my thesis in the future. Anyone who cannot concede this conveniently qualified point is not a

31

person worth knowing. I will not belabor its greatness here because there are only two types of people in the world (to crib a little Yeats): people who love "Bohemian Rhapsody", and people who have yet to hear "Bohemian Rhapsody."

I can understand the appeal of a song like that to a person in Kanye West's position. He makes his nut by playing arenas and produces music designed to be experienced in those venues (which is why his later albums are so simple and vapid). When you play arenas, there's an expectation of spectacle, and West usually delivers the ridiculous goods here. (Note: I use "goods" in the supply and demand sense, not the qualitative sense.)

His relentlessly shit rendition of "Bohemian Rhapsody"—which largely consists of him bobbing to the original track and getting the audience to take over the actual singing—is so bad that it crosses into actual offense.

The concert at which this desecration took place should have been stopped, the DJ murdered at his turntable rig, choked until his eyes popped out of his skull by his headphone cord, clenched in the twirling fists of slavering roadies while the audience descended in a frenzied rage upon the stage to rend Kanye West limb from misbegotten limb, carrying his various body parts out of the arena and into the streets, where people chucked them against billboards and shoe store displays in an attempt to scrub the defilement from their collective memory until all that is left is a quivering, pulp-covered earpiece microphone, through which hums the white, teeming silence of knowing electricity and justice dispatched.

Prince doesn't really do covers on his albums, ever. He slides other people's songs into his live shows like anybody else, but when he does it you know it's because he's making a point—educating the audience, some jamming fun with the band, etc.—not because his setlist needs the help. He's got enough problems trying to release hundreds of his own songs before they rot away that he doesn't have to borrow anyone else's. He is not a fan of the cover, and he doesn't like it when people cover his music. He prefers artists to go their own way.

All that said, when he does cover a song, it's good and damned covered. Case in point: "Betcha by Golly, Wow." This classic tune originally recorded by The Stylistics back in 1972 appeared as a bit of a shock on Prince's three LP album, *Emancipation*. Prince just didn't do covers. Nearly every Prince record before it was stamped with the assurance that he had written, produced, played, arranged, performed and engineered almost everything on a given album, and here we were, confronted with an album with four covers (the others being "La La La Means I Love U" (sic) by The Delfonics, "I Can't Make You Love Me" by Bonnie Raitt, and "One of Use" originally recorded by Joan Osborne). And he smashed "Betcha by Golly, Wow," so much so that it was an official release from the album with a (so-so) video and everything. He sang all the parts, which basically means he turned into The Stylistics. You know, because he can actually sing almost every note on a piano.

7) Kanye wants to break into fashion. Prince embodied fashion.

Kanye once said God told him to wear a kilt because his leather pants were too tight. This is a dude who put on a runway show full of clothing that looked like his baby cut them by hand. We're talking about someone—a black someone—who tried to make a Confederate flag an accessory (and merchandise). You know, to re-purpose it. You know, because "nigga" worked out so well. He blew up on Sway's radio show after being asked why he wasn't succeeding in the fashion game. His response? Race card (from the guy who thinks racism is "silly," mind you). Oh, and throwing yet another famous tantrum for the books. Like, top 5 tantrums of all time.

And then there's Prince, who, for much of the 80s, was an actual fashion style. He didn't make statements; he put on clothing and then thousands of people raided thrift stores in attempts to copy him before they went to their respective nightclubs in mascara and jheri curl pompadours.

Prince's ultimate fashion test? At the end of the day, no one should be able to survive performing at an awards show in a pair of pants with the ass buns cut out. It's the kind of thing only Prince could do. It may not seem very racy now, in the full blush ignorant bliss that is 2015, but think about it: how many people have done it since then? A handful, tops. Only Prince could do it and it not a) seem desperate (which anybody attempting the stunt after him probably can't say), and b) ruin his career. The man's fashion is completely alien and nonsensical, and yet completely unassailable.

8) *Sign O' The Times* **vs.** *College Dropout*

It's a pretty straight-forward equation: greatest offering versus greatest offering, winner is the greatest. This wouldn't be a question worth answering, but L.A. Reid is making me, so we press on.

College Dropout is arguably Kanye's best record. I'm not as enamored of *Dropout* as most, but I see its merits, particularly in the context of its time. Kanye had been producing tracks for other artists (many of which he should have kept for himself) and his debut was more of an extension of what he was already known for instead of being representative of an out-of-the-blue new artist. Rap being what it was in early 2004, who can blame audiences for the hype it received? There hadn't been a lot of mainstream rap albums released around the time West's debut dropped (February), and 2004 turned out to be a weak year in general. 2004 only turned out about one good rap record per month, maybe, and rap by that point was so underwhelming we were treated to the fifth posthumous 2Pac record just in time for Christmas (you know, in case anyone wanted to give half-baked, unfinished remix demos to someone they loved).

Comparing West's best record to Prince's best record—and again, context—I can tell you right now this part will go quick.

First, we have to decide which of Prince's records is the "best," defined here as the album that a) is most representative of the abilities of the artist at a peak, b) has the most songs showcasing as much, and c) is generally recognized as being at least a good, if not great record.

It's hard to determine that for Prince because you have to narrow down from a handful of classic albums to one. You have to decide between *1999*, *Purple Rain* or *Sign O' the Times*. I've thought about this a lot and based on some metrics, I've determined the following:

- *1999* is the most Prince album ever.
- *Purple Rain* is his greatest album.
- *Sign O' the Times* is his best album.

If someone who had never heard of Prince wanted to know what all the fuss was about, you could put on any of these records, but if you put on *1999* the neophyte will wait until the needle bounces into the final groove of the second LP, look at you with tears in their eyes and ask you to play it all over again, such will be their devotion to Prince. *1999* will make you fan; a dancing, singing in the shower, let me light this candle my dear fan. *1999* is what the color purple sounds like when it's having sex.

Purple Rain is the album that cemented Prince in history. *1999* was amazing, but *Purple Rain* showed he could do the magic more than once, and in different ways. *1999* made him famous, while *Purple Rain* made him a god amongst stars.

Sign O' the Times is the record all the critics love and just makes these conversations easier to have with white people. The quality of its genre spread is amazing, and by that point it was clear that Prince could do anything. It is the album that has his best efforts spread across the most genres of music. It is the album that shows you what kind of art he is capable of. So *Sign O' the Times* it is.

This is the part where I normally insert a spreadsheet breaking down the tracks and what-not, but in light of the fact that I had to narrow down Prince's numerous legendary albums to figure out which one I would use to make a case against West's easily-picked solitary offering, I'm going to give my fingers a break and let the question speak for itself.

Just remember: *Sign O' The Times* > *College Dropout*.

9) Prince pimps the music industry hard. Kanye largely remains an industry tool.

Remember *Musicology*? Prince hadn't had a real hit record in a long time, so he made a pimpin' decision and came up with a way to turn the industry's hype machine against itself: he "sold" copies of his new album, *Musicology*, with tickets at his live shows, which were counted as sales of the album. The trick gave Prince his first platinum record in years, and was so cunning that Billboard and Soundscan changed their rules for sales determination moving forward. The icing on the cake, of course, was that the album was actually good, netting Prince two Grammys wins that year, with three more nominations as a side dish. The Grammys are largely a critical wash, but can still generate a lot of buzz for sales, and Prince happened to crack that formula coming and going.

Kanye? Kanye is a firm product of the industry. His idea of working the hype machine is to be as grotesquely narcissistic as possible, which most of the people who don't buy his records will tell you is half the reason they don't buy his records: no matter how they feel about his music, they simply can't stomach handing over good money to someone so ridiculously sophomoric. And while he does great business despite such finger-wagging, he could be doing so much more. He hasn't crossed the line of no return yet—the point at which the mere sight of him in a headline will generate more revulsion that interest—but he's due. For someone who's only been in the game a little over a decade, that's a pretty fast burn-out.

10) Is Kanye even great?

When the movie *The Equalizer* came out last year I was skeptical of its merits. My main issue (of which there were a few) was with the casting of Denzel Washington in the lead. Let's be clear: Denzel is a fine actor. One can quibble with the stock in which he chooses to invest the use his talents, but one cannot watch fare like *Power*, *Malcolm X* and *Training Day* and not marvel at the intensity he is capable of generating when the material rises to the occasion of his abilities.

All that said, Denzel is an actor who is too aware of how he is perceived by the public and frequently caters to the impression of himself as an upstanding classy black woman catnip, a sort of high-end self-imposed typecasting. It is an impression that graduated long ago to brand, and it flavors the projects that he chooses to do and what those projects become capable of once he is attached: the pulled punches, the scenes he will not do, the words he will never say. Eventually all those pulled punches add up. Eventually, you draw a line in the sand so wide no one is willing to jump it to get to you for fear of discovering you're not going to give them what they want.

In short, you can hit your brand too hard.

Kanye West is a brand, a product in the starkest and most base sense of the word. That we at times may find him entertaining is a byproduct of what he does, not his goal. But West's problem isn't that his brand is stuck in a musical groove; it's that it's stuck in a behavior groove.

West has a sincere and clear desperation to be great. Not, mind you, to be a better musician or to be a better producer or to have the best albums or videos in a given year. He's not dedicated to actually doing any of those things. He has, however, doubled down on his attempts to convince us that these are happening. You can hear it in his whining, his meltdowns, his rants, his mumbling. They won't let me in. They won't give me what they give other designers. My clearly untalented wife will be the next Beyonce. All desperation.

For all the talk about the daring of his artistic risks and the scope of his vision, half of his proclamations aren't original, and the other half are eventually exposed for the half-baked ideas they are. On this front his albums *808 and Heartbreaks* and *Yeezus* stand as the most damning evidence.

Regarding the first, for which only the public can be blamed, much was made of his attempt to capture the zeitgeist of electronic emo soul with *808s & Heartbreaks,* as if no rapper before had ever attempted to brave such vast wastelands, as if no one had ever heard of Lauryn Hill or Bone Thugs-N-Harmony; as if Andre 3000 hadn't drawn the paint-by-numbers outline for Kanye's entire catalogue for him five years before with *The Love Below*; as if Mos Def's *The New Danger*—an album West was at least in the orbit of—hadn't shown an earnest way of incorporating singing into your rap career four years before; as if The Foreign Exchange hadn't just released *Leave It All Behind* the month before *808s* came out.

Understand, these are not charges against Kanye directly. Anyone can put out bad or unoriginal music and claim it to be the best record of the year. An artist doesn't generate their own greatness. Greatness is awarded. No, these are charges against those who claim greatness on his behalf, who proclaim him king of a mountain already climbed—and in some cases, still sat upon—by pre-existing royalty. I forgive that portion of his audience that is young, that cannot largely be expected to look beyond what is in front of them because that is what it means to be young. But I cannot as easily forgive the same from people who know better, who have seen these examples and more, yet still proclaim West to be an adequate torchbearer of such vision.

Here is something about West even I cannot dispute: he is one of the bestselling artists in music. He is clearly capable of making music that people are willing to spend money on. He is great at hype. He is great at moments. But he is not patently, inarguably, eternally, artistically great.

As I write this, the internet is a-boil with discussions about whether or not Drake used a ghostwriter on some songs, courtesy of an accusation by Meek Mill, who needs a ghostwriter on most songs. The interesting part of this kerfuffle (because a rap beef between Drake and anyone is automatically degraded from beef to vegetarian by-product on principle) is how willfully ignorant audiences remain about the productivity of superstar rappers.

West's average number of producers is two (including himself) and after his third release his albums begin to explode with co-writers (and not just the typical sample credit he has to give for the plethora of songs he borrows from). His last few albums have yielded a handful of producers per track…a far cry from the lone credits he assumed for his first record. The albums are so farmed out that no one really bothers arguing if he is the best producer in rap, not for some years now. No one bothers arguing if he is the best rapper in the genre, not sincerely. Not even close. We all know the answer: there are too many other rappers that are clearly better at doing it, and that's before you start pulling hungry rappers without record deals off the street. There are better mainstream rappers than Kanye West. There are more dexterous and clever rappers; rappers with more compelling subject matter and stronger vocabularies and a hundred times more earnest. The disparity between Kanye case by case begs we investigate why we ask the question of his greatness that way at all. If he isn't the best at anything, what is it that makes him so great?

West is the emblematic of the type of accidental celebrity that can consume the public mind these days, and for largely the same reasons. The fairer question would be, how is he different at this point in his life from Flavor Flav at the height of his VH1 madness? Why, when his music is at its laziest and least compelling, are we still comparing him to great musicians at all?

And now we arrive at the fatal logic of the Kendrick Lamar Hurdle.

If, for some reason, after all these many words, Prince isn't getting the job done for you—because he's not rap, because he's old, because he hasn't put out a great record in a long time, whatever—we still must wrestle with the Kendrick Lamar Hurdle. We're not comparing random no-deal rappers to West now. Now we are comparing him to someone who is firmly in the game and uncontestably at the top of it. Every artistic thing that can be said about Kanye West by his acolytes applies double for Kendrick Lamar off of *To Pimp a Butterfly* alone. Kendrick is a better rapper than West in every way by leagues—vocabulary, flow, engaging subject matter, production value, musicality, originality. *To Pimp a Butterfly* is better than at least 80% of West's output, if not all of his output. As influential as some of West's work might be—even to Lamar—it cannot withstand a track-by-track weighing of their merits when faced with the personally uncompromising and political juggernaut that is *Butterfly*. It is an album—not a song, but an entire record—you will be playing five years from now, and talking about for ten. Can the same be said just four years after *Watch the Throne*? I firmly believe that Kanye's long-hinted *SWISH* album is constantly being delayed because better music keeps coming out before it, and *Butterfly* probably set West back a year. If *SWISH* comes out in 2015 at all it will be too soon, and not just because I won't like it.

So to be clear:
Everyone knows he's not the best rapper.
Everyone knows he's not the best producer.
Everyone knows he can't play an instrument.
Everyone knows he doesn't sell the most records.
Everyone knows he doesn't produce the best videos.
Everyone knows his attempts at fashion are laughable.

Even taken collectively, he hits most of these fields at a below average level. All of these observations are practically empirical. So what is it exactly that's supposed to be so great about Kanye West?

Kanye West is not any of the coddling euphemisms that journalists and fans like to use to mask their lack of objectivity. He is also not a "lightning rod;" he paints targets on himself intentionally. He is not misunderstood; he is juvenile. He is not an unheralded genius; he is an overrated narcissist. He is not great; he is popular. He is not standing up for artists' rights; he is a complete tool of the market. He is not bravely outspoken; he is a spoiled anti-intellectual. He is not the best at anything he does; he is merely hip to the maxim that all press is good press. In light of the evidence I would argue that, as an artist, he isn't great at all.

And on no day of the week in any year is he, nor will he ever be, as great as Prince.

Acknowledgements

In this endeavor I must thank the following people, without whose cold hard cash this treatise would not be possible. I like to think of them collectively as the WTF Group—Woods Trust Fund Group—though that's mostly just a slick handle for a Kickstarter cabal: Mike Alcock, Anil Dash, Amy David, Chanda Green, Gabriel Israel Green, Glen Kizer, Sam Mercer, Mike (last name unknown), Bob Nelson, Amanda Page, Ed Plunkett, Oulanje Regan, Louise Robertson, Kelly Stumbaugh, and Rob Sturma. I also want to thank the various people who saw early versions of this and offered suggestions. Thank you all. It's all their fault.

RECLAIMING THE BLACK PRINCE
(2018)

Much of what we know about Prince prior to the advent of the internet comes from print sources: magazine articles, choice interviews, a dozen or so books of varying quality, and much of it draws from the same pool of associates. A lot of how he has been perceived by the public at large, Prince fan or otherwise, comes from a handful of anecdotes and images from a small window of his career, the early to mid-eighties. It is self-defined mythology, a new breed religion whose bible chapters are albums, a strictly approved gospel of photographs, and a pulpit-slamming legal team hammering down anything not owned or consented by Prince. The thing that eventually stood out to me as a black writer and fan was something that is rarely discussed, or rather poorly debated: that Prince scholarship is a canon largely written and maintained by white people. The issue isn't whether or not this is true. The issue is why this is occasionally a problem.

Thanks to social media, things in the world of Prince scholarship are a little different now, but not by much. There is more information to be had than ever before, which is a boon for fans of every level, but the infrastructure of access to that information remains virtually unchanged. Books about Prince remain largely written by whites. The majority of Prince's audience is still white, particularly high ticket fans and collectors. Journalism is still largely white. Academic scholarship is still largely white, and remains so because academia is perennially white. If the people who participate in the burgeoning Prince conference market or maintain hundreds of online forums dedicated to Prince or attend annual Celebration events at Paisley Park each year are any indication, Prince has more white fans than any other type. I haven't crunched all of the particulars on this, but I don't think anyone who has ever been to a Prince concert outside of Detroit would fight me over the data. More, none of this is particular to Prince, even as a black artist; just ask any rapper with a record deal. Any American artist who sells a hundred million records over the course of their career has done so on the backs of many white dollars. And to be clear, there's nothing inherently wrong with Prince-ing while white.

These realities are, however, unaddressed parts of the foundation of what has become the largest fight about Prince since his death: who gets to establish the legacy of Prince?

Ideally, everyone who encountered his music would get to determine his legacy through a conceptual ownership of his work, buying new product as it is released, and using a combination of scholarship and social media to democratically direct and engage the work critically through suggestion, review, and analysis. Some of this is happening in Prince fan circles, though the effect on the market has yet to bear much fruit. The projects that have come out since his death so far were predictable affairs, and contained things many fans already had access to years ago (albeit illegally and of poor quality). We've yet to see the Prince project that feels truly fresh or, more importantly, genuinely expands his legacy. The recently released *Piano and a Microphone 1983* album is nice to own without worrying about lawyers creeping into your hard drive, but is mostly a footnote to the Prince we already know, not a new branch on the tree that is his catalog. If he didn't have several tons of material in a vault, the question of his legacy would be easy: we'd have what he released, whatever anecdotes came with that body of work, maybe a couple of unreleased things of note, and then we'd put him on the shelf next to The Beatles and Michael Jackson and move on. With Prince, such closure is impossible with the knowledge that so much material remains to be explored, some of it sure to rival music we know and love. You can't cap even a 50+ album career knowing there are hundreds of songs slowly peeling away on plastic tapes somewhere. As a Prince superfan, it is hard to sleep some nights knowing there might be enough material out there to piece together, if not *Purple Rain*, another *Diamonds and Pearls* or even another *The Gold Experience*.

The ideal situation described above is standard operating procedure for how the legacies of white artists are handled, owing largely to the fact that much of the press, scholarship and fandom of a white artist are comprised of white people speaking to other white people. When the artist is black, however, most of the same interested parties—press, scholarship, industry, maybe fans, maybe most of the fans - are still white, but now they speak with a cultural agency they may have little to no actual experience with. White people don't create all the art, but they get to write all the books and most of the reviews and speak at all of the conferences. They get to do all of the contextualizing of the artist and their work, essentially informing the rest of us what's worth codifying or preserving, what's good, and how it got to be worthy of their attention.

You may be wondering why I feel the need to bring race into this at all. That's easy: I'm bringing race into this because legacy is how we define culture, and culture is how we define what kind of society we will be.

As an interrogator of all things Prince, all of the admittedly broad statistics above might be my problem, but they weren't Prince's problem. Prince spent the majority of his career straddling the camps of white and black audiences with his art, sometimes with a one-two punch of divergent-sounding releases aimed to draw in key demographics, like Prince followed by Dirty Mind. Sometimes that fishing happened within the same album, like 1999's side three white-genre-facing New Wave/electronica/rock ballad three-piece ("Automatic"/"Something in the Water"/"Free") followed by the bubbling funky (read black)-as-hell fourth side ("Lady Cab Driver" /"All the Critics Love U In New York"/"International Lover"). What's interesting about determining his success in this regard is noting how any barriers he may have faced had less to do with him or his music and more with whatever baggage audiences brought to the table.

Broadly speaking, black audiences that listen to and buy mainstream music tend to determine what we like first by what looks and sounds like us. The bulk of that decision is cultural—survival, really—and some of it is the market boxing in the playing field, limiting options along traditional radio lines. When black artists deviate from black audience expectations of them, we ratchet down support, or move on to someone else, maybe even something else if the change is broad enough (say, from blues to rock). Unfortunately, we have not traditionally spent a lot of time considering the cultural implications of letting whole art forms go, even when we create them…perhaps because we've proven over and over again that we can just make another art form when it suits us. It is how we lost ownership and an appreciation of both the blues and jazz to white audiences and power brokers. This bridge-too-far hurdle black audiences often apply to music is ultimately how we collectively missed the latter half of Prince's career, revisiting him on occasion like a long-lost cousin fresh from a stint in prison during funky musical spikes like "Sexy MF" or *Musicology*. Black folks give culture away like we're criminals on the run who can't afford to get caught with too much weight. And if we are completely honest, we almost gave Prince away too. Almost.

White popular music audiences generally treat black music differently. Their cultural investment in it is different, with many priding themselves on their ability to consume and even absorb any type of music...the key word here being "absorb," not "appreciate." The difference between the two is why blues sales charts are filled overwhelmingly with young white artists and their audiences almost entirely with old white men. There are a multitude of reasons why those kind of shifts occur—some intensely cultural (desegregation), some nudged along or out entirely by technology (access to musical technology, venues, and studios), all driven by markets (radio ghettoization, urban music departments)—but happen they do, and Prince spent forty years of his life navigating that strait, mining it for its multicultural riches.

Unfortunately, the question of Prince's legacy—and some of it is still very much a question—is where the cultural differences in his audiences come to a distasteful head. There are a number of ways in which these cultural differences contribute to undermining the work of legacy building, but most manifestations fit under one action item: white fans frequently attempt to strip Prince of his blackness.

How this stripping occurs depends on what kind of problematic white Prince fan we're talking about. In my experience they fall into one of two camps: the fan who suggests Prince's work beyond his clearly black moments owes a grand debt to white musical influences almost exclusively; and the fan who suggests that Prince's blackness is irrelevant next to his larger messages (with a wild branch of fan who thinks Prince isn't black at all).

The first camp can be hard to recognize for two reasons. First, many of these fans are the writers and scholars of Prince minutiae, so we're inclined to give them more credit because they write for major magazines or have published books. We assume they know more than everyone else, and in a few cases their behind-the-scenes credentials are indeed legitimate. People tend to vet them less because their fandom is deemed almost professional.

Also, their manifestations of this issue are more subtle, imbued with a near shade-like quality. They think Prince's indisputable abilities are overly influenced by the trailblazing of white artists, almost exclusively. Bob Dylan, The Beatles, David Bowie, and Joni Mitchell are common references in their determinations. When they speak of influential black artists they are often the black artists that white artists have already namechecked as influences for themselves: James Brown, Sly Stone, Jimi Hendrix, Little Richard. These fans generally understand how musicianship works, at least enough to know that there are no unicorns in music, and understand that every musician listens to someone, usually several someones, and anyone as good as Prince at both playing and composing likely listened to hundreds of someones. And yet, they treat Prince as if he was a bedroom savant all his life that one day poked his head out of the ground like a guitar-wielding groundhog, or an accidentally smart pet; a genius, sure, but untouched by musical influence save for random meetings with hip white people who broadened his palate. Producer/songwriter Chris Moon and bandmates Wendy Melvoin and Lisa Coleman are the most popular designees here, but hardly alone. To them, Prince is a talented sponge of music, but of white music first, unwilling to conceive of a direction for his music or career without the touchstones of white artists or the largesse of white guides.

Prince came from a regional scene that was massively talented, musically diverse, and predominantly black. Bands like Haze, Flyte Tyme, Prophets of Peace, The Family (no, not that one), and, of course, 94 East worked the clubs (many of which were still essentially segregated), had their records spun at local parties, exchanged band members and instruments…all things Prince was accessing as an up-and-coming musician. There may be no greater benefit to be derived from the 2013 Numero Uno collection, *Purple Snow*, than finally exposing not only the kind of music Prince was constantly surrounded by and contributing to, but the blackness as well. Prince was an active participant in Minneapolis' black culture as he learned to play and develop his musical ideas. Even at two jam-packed discs, *Purple Snow* represents only a smattering of the acts that tilled the soil from which Prince would share experiences and later, musicians.

One of the most expensive records a collector of Prince memorabilia can acquire is an original vinyl copy of the self-titled album, *The Lewis Conection* (sic). The album features the song "Got To Be Something Here," and is notable for being one of the earliest recordings of Prince legally available. Recorded two years before Prince's debut, he only sings background and plays guitar on the track. Compared to the playing and production values we know Prince for it's not outstanding—he is essentially a session player here—but the album stands as clear testimony to the type of environment in which Prince was subsumed. He jammed, recorded, and composed alongside local bands of extreme diversity in style and talent, almost all of whom were black. This type of local research can be done and applied effectively, as is done in the excellent (and aptly named) book, *Got To Be Something Here: The Rise of the Minneapolis Sound* (2107) by Andrea Swensson. If more Prince researchers took the time to, if not commit the same level of hustle as Swensson, at least reference the work that's been done that broadens our understanding of his world, the bar of the entire field could be raised.

Most Prince investigations also doesn't focus much on other reference points that would have been commonplace for a black musician coming up in the late 1960s and through the 1970s. Prince's obvious influences always get their shine (James Brown, Parliament/Funkadelic, etc.), even from him. And sure, he tried to convince people that he didn't listen to other people's music early on to improve his boy-wonder stock, but most people recognize that such claims were a fabrication, and half the musicians who worked the Minneapolis scene would certainly tell you otherwise. You can't listen to Ernie Isley's guitar solo on "Summer Breeze" from The Isley Brother's 1973 album *3+3* and not envision a then fifteen-year-old Prince trying to play along, or hear the influence in his own style of playing. Ernie Isley probably spontaneously generated a thousand black guitar players in 1973 alone. Not enough is made of how much of Prince's music sounds like the rest of the black music that was happening all over not only Minneapolis, but the country at that time. Prince's first two albums have liberal hints of Cameo, The Ohio Players, Sylvester, and dozens of other black bands that were prominent at the time. If you're a person who believes Prince created either of those albums in a self-referential vacuum, then you've never listened to a Switch album or heard of Shuggie Otis (also a wunderkind multi-instrumentalist who released his first album at 17 in 1970). How many Prince songs sound like Otis' song "Special"? Answer: more than a few, and while not released until much later, the song is indicative of the kind of music that was happening on and off the record everywhere, including while Prince was finding his way. Much has been made of Prince's rivalry with Michael Jackson but very little of the conversation considers how a decade of Jackson 5 hits influenced a generation of black musicians in the 1970s, including—and perhaps especially—Prince.

The problem with the way white-based scholarship tends to navigate Prince's roots isn't that its adherents are unaware of this information; they just don't think it's important or relevant. Even in what is perhaps the most comprehensive (and at over 600 pages, longest) Prince biography, Matt Thorne's *Prince* (reprinted in 2016), gives short shrift to the period Prince spent developing his craft in Minneapolis. Of the 600 pages that comprise Thorne's tome, only ten cover Prince's formative years as a working, growing musician on the Minneapolis scene before he is taken in under the wing of Chris Moon.

Imagine a scenario in which a similar dismissal of cultural influence was leveled against, say, The Beatles. Can you imagine a version of The Fab Four without having weathered Liverpool's music scene? Or Elvis without the influence of his beloved (and black) Memphis? Or The Beach Boys without the muse that is California surf culture? To suggest that any of these artists created in a cultural vacuum would be offensive, yet Prince is regularly stripped of these influences.

The bands Prince worked with, learned from, and revered don't come up very often in research about him because white fans remain largely ignorant of either their existence or their relevance. I am willing to give them enough leeway to suggest that the dismissal isn't willful, and that sometimes a blindspot is just a blindspot. At the same time, erasure isn't defined by the intent of the person holding the eraser, but by what goes missing. Applying a cultural context that accounts for Prince's race as a matter of course and not a footnote—or worse, irrelevant—broadens our ability to appreciate and interpret his music, as well as piece together a more interesting, honest, and complete picture of his history, ideas, and values. Contextualizing Prince as black does not undermine his image or genius; it expands those things.

Which brings us to the second camp of problematic white fans, the ones who commit the crime of identity erasure.

This group of fans has less of a leg to stand on logically, and conversely their issues are far more politically repellent. This type of fan casually strips away Prince's ethnicity as if becoming a colorless being was his goal, or worse, this somehow improves his standing as a cultural icon. It is clear how Prince muddied this water early in his career but I'm here to tell you what every real fan should have learned by now: Prince told people what they wanted to hear so that they would give his music a chance. If he had to exoticize himself by suggesting his parents weren't black, fine; he would, for a while, become your quadroon or part-Italian mix fantasy if it would make the uncomfortable image of a black man with a guitar take a backseat to the music he was creating. While Prince was using no small amount of political and cultural shorthand, he was ultimately not attempting to transcend race so much as make it a non-factor in how people considered whether or not to listen to his music. It is the same principle ground into the heels of every civil rights marcher. Prince was attempting to sell a post-racial religion to a firmly committed racist society, not because race was unimportant, but because it was wrong to tell audiences what they should listen to on the basis of his skin color alone.

This non-existent need by black people to be seen as colorless is a political distinction white America has always projected onto the goal of the work blacks do in the name of self-preservation and justice. It is a historical mistake baked into every layer of America's perception of not only race, but freedom. White people think that black people want to be their friends as part of the mission of freedom, when in fact the goal is to level up the freedoms we're already supposed to have. If we have to be friendly to be able to eat, fine, we'll be friendly. It might even take. We have certainly made worse concessions in the name of survival while waiting for white folks to catch up to an awareness of our actual needs. But black folks would much rather be able to do what white people take for granted every day: decide on a case by case basis if we want to be bothered with the world and it not potentially get us fired, maimed or killed because we weren't living to code.

These black concessions are all tools Prince used in the interest of disseminating his art and advancing his career. As an album, *Controversy* is perhaps his most bald challenge to expose the cultural hypocrisy of not only radio and music industry forces, but of audiences themselves, forcing the question of what freedom and equality really meant and questioning how far we were willing to go to make our case. He did this visually in the doctoring of his look on the album cover (a little off the nose and lips, please) and in the ethnic composition of his bandmates (though it bears pointing out that the black players were up front and the white players were all but behind the fog machines). He did this in the mash-up of thrift/gay/WTF fashion styles, while courting secular versus religious imagery in accompanying videos. He did this sonically in the blending of new wave, funk, and punk music styles. He even challenged the English language, this album marking his first use of what would become a career-long fascination with sensational spelling in his song titles. *Controversy* is Prince's post-racial/sexual/religious playbook, and he would return to its Xs and Os over and over again until white people got on board.

Fans in this camp love pointing to what they perceive as the smoking gun at the core of his colorless philosophy: the lyrics to the titular song of the album. The lyrics of "Controversy" have, over the years, become the chief exhibit of people seeking to strip Prince of his blackness, philosophically or literally. They point to a number of lines in the song, but the two they hone in on with the fervor of a zealot are:

"Am I black or white, am I straight or gay?"
…and
"I wish there was no black and white, I wish there were no rules."

These lines lay out his essential racial truth, they say, or in less dire cases, they suggest that Prince did not think the question of whether or not he was black was important. Several interesting glitches pop up in the matrix of this logic:

It is interesting that, despite the query of "Am I black or white, am I straight or gay?", no one thinks Prince was gay, yet the same line is somehow evidence that he was on the fence about his blackness, or that he wasn't "just" black at all.

It is interesting that, despite stating what he wished were a cultural reality, Prince was keenly aware of the political reality in which he lived in every other way, being a twenty-two-year-old streetwise black man living in Minneapolis, a city that in 1980 only had 370,000 people in it, of which only 48,000 were black.

It is interesting that this supposedly colorblind Prince was the same Prince who was booed off the stage nearly twice by 93,000 people in Los Angeles while opening for the Rolling Stones three days before the release of *Controversy*, an experience loaded with racial aggression and violence, traumatizing Prince to the point of leaving the first show on a plane back home, having to be coaxed back to Los Angeles to do the second almost-aborted show. Ah, if only the band would have called an audible and fired up "Controversy." I'm sure that would have changed everything.

When he belts out the line "we don't need no race" in "Sexuality," it isn't a suggestion delivered for his benefit, but a demand for white people to get hip. Unfortunately, many white fans have interpreted this and similar sentiments as manifestos for a colorblind world. It is not a wholly unreasonable interpretation of the meaning of the lyric, but it is ridiculous to hold the lyric up as a reality for Prince or anyone else.

For the record, no black person has ever transcended race. Some black people have obscured their race to pass for something else, but that isn't transcendence so much as it is a survival mechanism. Prince may have convinced a reporter to suggest to their audience to fight for a world where race was less relevant in deciding how we might interact with one another, but he operated personally under no illusions that he was anything other than black, and later in his life made this even clearer in his music, philanthropy, and public statements. Prince regularly tossed conflicting personal information into interviews to obfuscate his image, not clarify his reality.

Black audiences heard the same lyrics white people did, but we didn't take them to mean he was going proto-Tiger Woods on us. We understood what Prince was doing; he was code-switching, telling white people what they wanted to hear ("I wish there was no black and white") to get what he needed from them (white sales). Being right or talented or wearing the right clothes isn't enough to survive being black in a white society. In this respect, Prince lived up to the two oldest black adages since we hit American shores: work twice as hard for the same reward, and know more than one language. Prince was a shining example of both tactics at work in his quest to level the field enough to be able to do what he wanted as an artist.

Prince's blackness bled through all of his transformations and mission statements. His music has passed through all of the officially recognized Black Uncle phases. Conversely, Prince has been, at one time or another:

- the cool black uncle who slipped you your first taste of something you were too young to have ("Darling Nikki");
- the black uncle who hurts himself trying to show The Younguns that there is nothing new under the sun by attempting their dances ("Housequake");
- the trash talking black uncle who cannot lose at Spades ("Bob George");
- the black uncle who, upon his release from prison, got super religious ("The Cross");
- the black uncle who wears his work uniform at all times because he "got to work in the morning" ("Black Sweat");
- the black uncle who hits on your girlfriend ("International Lover");
- the black uncle who gets into a shouting match with his lady at every gathering for 30 years ("Man o War");
- the black uncle who tells you to cut out all that "gay shit" ("Bambi");
- the gay black uncle ("If I Was Your Girlfriend");

- the black uncle who thinks rap ain't shit ("Dead On It");
- the black uncle who follows just enough news to have developed conspiracy theories ("Annie Christian");
- the fat black uncle who rudely keeps pointing out you gained weight ("Cloreen Bacon Skin");
- and Uncle Preach, who, contrary to his title, doesn't go to church and whose religion is women or jobs or old music or all of the above because his religion is really advice and you are going to hear about it all every time you see him, sometimes twice in one sitting ("The Sacrifice of Victor," which might be his most culturally self-referencing song ever).

A note on Prince's hiring practices: For someone whose artistic mission is, according to the group of white fans currently on the table, to live in a colorless world, his bands and protégés were overwhelmingly black. Of the ten most well-known backing bands and side projects that Prince created—Apollonia 6, Vanity 6, New Power Generation, the 1979-1983 band, the 1987-1989 band, Madhouse, The Revolution, The Family, The Time, and 3rdEyeGirl—he employed roughly 78 musicians, singers and dancers. Of the people he put on stage with him, only about 24 of them were white, less than a third. Having the opportunity and means to hire anyone he wanted for much of his career, Prince made it a point to hire and maintain predominantly black bands. While many factors may contribute to the hiring of a band, the one factor we know that Prince was always concerned with were the optics of his personnel. His bands reflected the values he wished to convey from project to project, but even when his messaging was not exclusively about race he made it a point to put forth a virtual musical army of black people. Any person who thinks Prince did not consider how such practices might be interpreted either underestimates the degree to which Prince controlled his image, or is a logic-masochist who simply likes to lose arguments.

No study of the influence of Prince's blackness in his work would be complete without mentioning the one project that, by all counts, should have been a colorblind slam dunk but became one of his blackest offerings ever: *Under the Cherry Moon*. Prince's second foray into cinema is a story featuring a comic and lewd version of himself that could have been played as colorless as the black and white film transfer itself. Instead, Prince proceeds to direct a film that is black as shit. Consider: the movie features two black-ass cats from Miami kicking it on the French Riviera, supported in large part by pimping Prince out to rich women. Jerome Benton has less of a wingman vibe and more a reformed pimp/gigolo thing happening. The two players jack white people for their money and largesse. They listen to Miles Davis and Sam Cooke records. They codeswitch and wear do-rags. They play a prank with black dialect on a spoiled classist. They commit an act of breaking and entering. Prince steals a Redd Foxx joke (the ugly people/ugly kid joke) and seduces a woman with open mic-level erotic poetry over the phone. And finally, they drive ridiculously pimped-out vehicles. *Under the Cherry Moon* is two steps away from being a blaxploitation flick.

(Aside: Should I even mention here the number of times Prince used the word "nigger" in a song? Or "nigga"? Or "niggah"? Prince used all of the variants, and in their culturally colloquial ways. You don't get to do that if you aren't black, period, ever, don't care what your black friend said. I could stop there and get on with my life, but then someone is going to mention how he used the word to sell records once he began experimenting with rap, and since he could kind of get away with it—which also means I could stop right there, but let's play the logic out—he put it in certain songs. To which I am forced to respond with the Piano and a Microphone 1983 recording of "17 Days", wherein he uses the word way back in 1983, not to incorporate it into a song, but as a black person often uses the word with themselves, earnestly, as an afterthought. In that solitary, unguarded moment, Prince reveals his composition process and his blackness.)

White fans are constantly making the case that Prince is an avatar of a colorless, post-racial world. Black people almost never make this case. To us, Prince is a black man who happens to wears boots, can get whatever woman he wants, and throws a great party. What's telling about people who make a case for the irrelevancy of Prince's blackness is that Prince was perfectly black until white people discovered him, or rather when he went in search of a white audience. Nobody was questioning his blackness when he was playing "I Wanna Be Your Lover" to 500 people and his opening acts were comedians back in 1980. That isn't the Prince whose ethnicity gets questioned. It is the Prince that white people know and like—but most importantly, that Prince caters to—that has the veracity of his ethnicity questioned.

Trying to ascertain why some white fans do these things is a study in and of itself that has very little to do with music and everything to do with the nature of whiteness and the society it has created to sustain itself. Many more pages would need to be added here to illustrate this point fairly, but would take us far afield of the original topic. What I can fit in here is the observation that whiteness is frighteningly normative. It is so structurally embedded in every facet of civilization that white people are more oblivious to the nature of their whiteness than non-whites. The average black person knows more about whiteness than the average white person. Consider that white people can go an entire day, week or month without considering the existence of their whiteness or, in many places, people of color. By contrast, black people have to be on the hook for knowing blackness and whiteness because our survival depends on it. A black person who doesn't consider white people in the wild potentially invites all manner of trouble. The blooming awareness of how frequently white people call the police on black people for just about any activity one can conceive of may be trending news for white people, but is a generations ancient reality for black people. Five years ago no one was talking about "white privilege" and now it's a more or less accepted footnote in media stories. A footnote, mind you, that isn't going anywhere and, contrary to what many Prince fans wish to believe, won't be stalled by playing *Graffiti Bridge* over and over.

Finally, nowhere in this essay am I suggesting that white people shouldn't write about Prince. Prince belongs to whomever finds him and can appreciate his work. I am, however, suggesting two things: 1) that more and consistent consideration be given to how Prince's blackness informs his work, and 2) that more effort be made to include the observations, interpretations, criticisms and work of black writers and fans into the body of research constantly being generated about him. At the end of the day, Prince was a middle-aged black dude born in 1958 in a post-segregated working class Midwestern city. He was a black man born to black parents six years before the Civil Rights Act became a law. He lived in a black neighborhood in a house run by a black woman and lived with his black best friend. He grew up playing black and white music in a predominantly black music scene in mostly black venues, and when he finally made it big, black music remained a significant part of the foundation of his work, which he mostly hired black musicians to play. Eventually he went on to commit acts of philanthropy in aid of black causes both musically and financially, and made the occasional public statement on black issues. And on April 21st in 2016, he died sporting the largest afro of his adult life. Prince was black, has always been black, and was proud to be black. Any narrative that dismisses, erases or otherwise strips those basic cultural realities from Prince does a disservice to him as an artist born of very specific traditions; to Prince as a human being possessing specific values and ideas, and to anyone who wants to know more about him and his work and how it might inform their own appreciation for his art, values, and ideas.

HOW U KNOW WHEN PRINCE LOVES U—
THE PRINCE SIDESTICK
(2015)

Prince's success across a wide range of styles is why we'll be talking about him in a hundred years, but isn't how most long-standing fans process his persona. Most people know Prince for a few key songs during impressionable points in their lives, or they're going to. He may have peaked thirty years ago, but his peak was so high he couldn't fall from it if he tried (and he's released plenty of albums to suggest that's a possible goal). Outside of the content and structure of the songs themselves, Prince's defining heyday sound (80s-90s) can best be boiled down to two distinct musical features, one obvious, the other less so: his screams (consisting of two particular versions: the "eye" scream and the "ouwa" scream) and the Prince Sidestick. Most people's favorite Prince song probably contains one of these two features. And yet, only the screams remain in his regular production toolbox, the Sidestick having done the work of cementing his sonic reign long ago.

Every great spoof or identifier of Prince's persona takes a shot at the first feature, but the second is equally important to deep analysis of his success. Prince was a genius at modifying the public's perception of who he was and what he was capable of, and his music was almost exclusively where much of that perception was handled. Identity was as important to his persona as the music, and these musical identifiers—one vocal, one technological—were key in making it easy for the public to draw their attention to what he was doing as an artist. It was a keen alchemy, and separated him from the pack beyond just writing singular songs. It was the weirdo icing on the fascinating cake.

I want to focus on the second element here—the Prince Sidestick. The screams are easy: you hear them, you know it's Prince, done deal. Left to my own devices one day, however, I began wondering when the sound first appeared in his catalog; the chunky knock that, for years, marked a Prince song as distinctly his, and despite its unique arrangement and amplification—or because of it—was rarely mimicked. It was a sound so steeped in Prince's aura that it marked one as a base imitator if it appeared in their music. Ready For The World, an 80s era R&B band that never heard a Prince riff it didn't mind shoving into a song, got off the ground by adhering as closely to his formula as possible. "Oh Sheila" is what happens when a bunch of dudes from Michigan think they can do "Lady Cab Driver" better. (Spoiler alert: no.) But they pretty much burned themselves by doing so and you'd be hard-pressed to find other acts that tried. The theory, sure. The sound itself? Why, who would bother?

That is a LOT of curl activator. This is what is known as a "metric buttload" of curl activator.

Controversy is the first great Prince record, and "Sexuality" is the first song that hips us to what Prince is capable of rhythmically, and lays the ground work for the sidestick, though it doesn't actually introduce the sound. Other songs on this record also lay the land for what's coming: "Annie Christian" unveils the kind of rhythmic opportunities that Prince would later use the sidestick in, and "Jack U Off" essentially uses a double-struck treated tom where Prince would later use the sidestick. The theory was there, his rhythms waiting for Prince to find the sidestick, turn the pitch knob on the LinnDrum, and hit that little black button to further cement his sound.

The rhythms only had to wait eleven months.

The first appearance of the Prince Sidestick is nine seconds into the song "1999," blending into the top of the tom fills so effortlessly one wonders why it's never happened before. When you hear it, you know you're in a Prince song. And he knew what he had, too: the sound appears on half of the songs on the *1999* album, and is a sound so quintessentially Prince—so key to defining and dog-earring his presence in the landscape of American pop music—that it kicks off the first song of the album that stands as the crowning achievement of his career, *Purple Rain*. In fact, of the nine songs that make up Purple Rain, six songs feature the sound. At the height of his powers and during the uncontestable breadth of his rule over the music world, the Prince Sidestick was a defining part of his palate, a subversive utensil in a toolbox designed to build the perfect pop star.

Its job done during *Purple Rain's* tenure, the Prince Sidestick fared less well as time marched on and Prince began almost immediately to reinvent himself (again) in an attempt to stay awake during the creative boredom that can set in with great success and being surrounded by sycophants. His next album, *Around the World In a Day*, set out to deconstruct the very image he'd spent the previous four years creating, and the titular Sidestick was a victim of that reformation. It appeared on only three songs noticeably: "Pop Life," "America" and "Raspberry Beret" (the singles, mind you). It hovers underneath the mix in "Temptation" almost imperceptibly, an afterthought on the final song of the record, mostly placed out of a need to fulfill a rhythmic hole than to enhance the song or define the artist. By the time his next film and album rolls around, it is all but gone, almost entirely replaced with explosively treated handclaps and toms reverbed until they were dripping with effect.

What the discerning listener will find interesting is that when he needs to re-establish himself or score a hit, he knows where the spice rack is. While the bulk of most of his records since *Purple Rain* feature tracks that don't use the sound, many of the standout tracks and hits from later records do. Prince knows when to apply the rub and when to let the song simmer…usually depending on what his career needs. He knows when to apply the magic to himself. When you hear the Sidestick, he's trying to get your attention, maybe even trying to meet you halfway past the lights and yes men.

Long live the Prince Sidestick. When he's using it, he's very likely thinking about you.

10 Songs That Feature The Prince Sidestick

1. 1999
2. Let's Go Crazy
3. When Doves Cry
4. Darling Nikki
5. Raspberry Beret
6. Delirious
7. Little Red Corvette
8. Something in the Water (Does Not Compute)
9. America
10. The Ballad of Dorothy Parker

THE ALBUMS PRINCE DIDN'T MAKE (BUT SHOULD HAVE)
(2017)

Every Prince fan thinks they know what Prince should have done better than him. There's no denying that his career had valleys, most of which were avoidable, and it's the avoidable moments that were most frustrating for longtime fans. Here we were running around the streets like a bunch of purple acolytes extolling the virtues of The Great Purple One, and he was attempting to fill holes in his relevancy with albums like *Rave Un2 the Joy Fantastic*. As a defense mechanism, Prince fans—unbeknownst to themselves as a group—developed a game called "If I Were Prince's Label..." The rules are simple: come up with album concepts or track lists that he could release that would cement the deal on one of his many attempts at a comeback. It's not a game in the sense that there's a winner at the end, especially considering none of our albums ever happened, and with his death, can't happen by his hand. (Come to think of it, it has now become someone's job to play this game for real.)

To wit, below are my top five entries when playing this game. It is known that Prince was considering at least one of these at some point in the past, but it never came to be because he disliked dealing with record companies, and any retrospective starts with a call to Warner Brothers. Alas.

The Ultimate Prince Slow Jam Album

The most common entry in this game, mostly because it's an easy one to come up with songs for that no one will argue over, and that every prince fan has already made in real life anyway. This is a concept that we know Prince actually spent some time on, but ultimately the project went nowhere. Ideally this would be a greatest hits collection that borrows from his entire career and some sexy unreleased material. Slow jams were his forte—he released dozens of them—so this is hard to get down to a manageable number of tracks. I narrowed it down to a two-album set of ten tracks apiece. (Also, not in order. The order of such music is an argument unto itself.)

1. Adore
2. Call My Name
3. Do Me, Baby
4. I Hate You
5. Insatiable
6. God (instrumental)
7. Joy In Repetition
8. June
9. How Come U Don't Call Me Anymore
10. Power Fantastic
11. Scandalous
12. Shhh
13. The Beautiful Ones
14. The Question of U
15. Venus De Milo
16. Slow Love
17. Elixir
18. When 2 R In Love
19. When We're Dancing Close and Slow
20. Somewhere Here on Earth

Honorable Mention: "International Lover," which is an incredible song, but is so ridiculous that you'd spend half of the time you thought you'd be making out laughing at how funny Prince is. And yet, sexy.

The Prince Hip Hop EP

Prince had what you might call an interesting relationship with rap. He didn't understand why people liked it, spent no small amount of time deriding it, then found some common ground with it. His efforts weren't always good, but he tried to figure it out (and on one song, finally cracked it).

1. Y Should Eye Do That When I Can Do This*
2. Sexy M.F.
3. Bob George

4.   My Little Pill
5.   Mr. Goodnight
6.   Valentina

* This is the most outstanding example of Prince rapping to be found. It works, it's funky, and the message is on point. This is what it sounds like when Prince approaches a thing he wants to critique out of respect instead of derision (see "Dead On It").

Prince: Legacy

This list is different from the previous entries in that it doesn't feature music Prince wrote or played. This is a legacy record, a "Butterfly Effect" experiment, assuming the butterfly in question is Prince. This is an album of songs that wouldn't exist without Prince; a record that, if you released it, every musician in existence would be forced to kneel whenever Prince entered a room. There are whole eras of music inspired by Prince, and most of the artists of the 80s were straight ripping his sound throughout the decade, so I had to install qualifiers. The caveat here is that the songs have to be ones I actually like, and I tried to stick to post-1990 songs unless they were creatively inspired (Terrence Trent D'arby "'Sign Your Name") and not a straight rip (George Michael "I Want Your Sex"; Natural Selection "Do Anything"; all of Ready for the World's first two albums). It's called "Legacy" not "CSI: Paisley Park."

1. D'Angelo "Untitled" (2000)

Few artists have made what they owe Prince more clear than D'Angelo. His first record hid this influence to some degree, but with the release of *Voodoo*, the cat was out of the bag. "Untitled" came out and half of the people who heard it for the first time thought it was a Prince song, and for good reason: it's a slow jam that mimics Prince so thoroughly D'Angelo should have cut him a check. It is the gold standard of how much a song can sound like someone you admire and still be yours. He had a more recent runner-up in "The Charade" from Black Messiah. To his credit, he's one of only about three artists that belong in front of a Prince tribute band.

2. Dornik "Strong" (2015)

This is the rare artist who has cracked the Prince/Michael Jackson combo in a way that doesn't make them feel plastic. He genuinely writes music that you believe either artist would make now if they were here. Production wise, "Strong" is basically a Prince song sung by Michael Jackson, down to the rapid fire toms and the lit high hat drills. Somewhere Bobby Z is either smiling at Dornik's drum work, or pissed.

3. Ne-Yo "Sex With My Ex" (2007)

I prefer when he's gunning for a Michael Jackson vibe, but this one stuck with me.

4. Miguel "NWA (feat. Kurupt)" (2015)

Miguel wants to be Prince so bad it hurts, and I feel for him because it's not going to happen. This track is like watching your buddy try to talk to a woman in a bar that's out of his league: you know nothing is going to happen, but you respect his balls.

5. The Foreign Exchange "Authenticity" (2010)

I know the musician responsible for the music for this band—Nicolay—is a huge Prince head because I've engaged him on multiple occasions about Prince. For this exercise, I picked the one song out of their five studio albums I thought might be the answer. Then I hit Nicolay up and asked what song he would pick. When he said "Authenticity" I laughed out loud. So of all the songs on this list, this one is empirically correct.

6. Bilal "White Turns to Gray" (2006)

The obvious choice here is "Soul Sista," but I wanted to have a few surprises on this list. In true Prince fashion, this excellent slow burn is from an album that didn't make it to the market and has been bootlegged ever since. I can't speak to the whole album, but this track is definitely inspired by our boy. And who is one of the few cats that can front a Prince tribute band and it be okay? Bilal.

7. The Dream "Fast Car" (2007)

8. Dam-Funk "Surveillance Escape" (2015)

Dam-Funk usually mines straight and hardcore funk as inspiration for his music, but this one is just about the most Prince-sounding jam that Prince didn't write I've heard in years. It's an unrelenting *Purple Rain*-era bit of irresistible funk that if I didn't tell you someone else wrote it, you'd think came out of Paisley Park in the 80s.

9. Bruno Mars "Uptown Funk" (2014)

This one pushes the limits of my qualifier a bit. First, the song is a riff on The Time's entire existence, which technically is Prince's funky side, so that much makes sense. But "Uptown Funk" has clear strains of Cameo in it, elements so much like them that I'm largely inclined to chalk this one up more to that funk unit than Prince some days. But today it's Prince.

10. Maxwell "Lifetime" (2001)

11. Childish Gambino—"Redbone" (2016)

This sounds like one of Prince's excursions into traditional soul, and is surprisingly engaging considering the source.

12. TLC "Waterfalls" (1994)

There are people in 2017 who still don't believe Prince didn't write this song.

13. New Sector Movements "Digital Age" (2004)

A broken-beat bit of techno funk whose vocals really put it firmly in Prince-sounding turf. The whiny falsetto with the "Erotic City" production value. A great song you wish Prince had it in him to do himself.

14. Jaguar Wright "I Can't Wait" (2001)

I mean, come on. I had to check to make sure this wasn't a Prince song, down to the vocals.

15. Tweet "Drunk" (2002)

This sister lifted this right out of his *1999* period, and the b-side vault at that. A great ballad about being drunk of all things. The strings are a dead Prince giveaway.

MICHAEL JACKSON VS. PRINCE:
WHO WAS THE "BEST"?
(2009)

Back in the early-80s, when Michael Jackson and Prince were at their professional peaks, they were the two most popular musicians in the world. The overlapping period in the peak of Michael Jackson and Prince's careers—1982-1984*—marked the release of each artist's sixth album, both dabbling in various genres and confounding record bin signage across the globe. MJ's release came with an outstanding series of groundbreaking videos, while Prince's was accompanied by a critically-lauded, hugely profitable film of which he was the star. Both of them had stellar live shows. Between the two of them, as well as the launching of hit TV show Miami Vice, nightclub fashion would never be the same again.

The world being what the world is, we had to rank them because, as you know, there simply can't be two great musical geniuses at once. Every week some newspaper was asking the question, "Who's the best?" Someone had to be the best, and that was that.

The question always bothered me. I liked them both, but thought them both different enough to make a question like "Who's the best?" seem inadequate. There isn't any single qualifying gauge that means anything between these two artists. Record sales? Please. We're talking about who is the "best," not how many lemmings would fill a good-sized pond. In some areas it was a fair question, but in other areas it was like comparing apples and high-heeled boots. If there is a best, they have to be the best at what they do, not what happens once they've done their jobs. They're not real estate salesmen; they're musicians. Not only do we need to define "best" better, but we need to break them down in categories so that one or the other is best at something (best live show, best music, best dance moves, best singer…you get the idea) and then determine perhaps which of them is the greatest pop star. Greatness might encompass things we can actually gauge, like influence or proficiency with professional hair gel products.

So I went into my laboratory, put on my lab coat and promised not to come out until I had the answer. It is as empirical an answer as I could manage, which is to say you are still unlikely to agree across the board.

Here's the math:

Influence + Catalogue + Business Acumen + Longevity + Grown Folks' Business + Songwriting + Sales + Live Performance + Musicianship + Je ne sais qua = Greatness

1) Prince is why we have Parental Advisory stickers.
Thanks to the fact that Tipper Gore's daughter didn't have the common sense to shut her bedroom door when she listened to songs about sex and masturbation, we've all been subjected to censorship that doesn't work anyway. That's a powerful song! MJ was always too pop to make waves like that.

Prince +1 Influence.

2) Prince is directly responsible for the infusion of sexual content in modern popular music.
Another gimme for Prince. All of that raunchy stuff you heard in the 90s were people trying to be Prince. You know how hard it was to make a good first impression when half the songs on your slow jam tape were by R. Kelly and Jodeci?

Prince +1 Influence, +1 Songwriting

3) *Thriller* broke every industry record there was.
…and remains the biggest selling record of all time 25 years later. Do I actually have to point out that this record will likely never be broken?

MJ +2 Influence, +2 Longevity, +1 Business Acumen, +5 Sales

4) MJ single-handedly changed what success in the music industry meant.
Prior to *Thriller*, a platinum record was possible, but no one had really hit the stratosphere in the then modern era. People who sold as many records as *Thriller* did typically did so after they died and over any more

years. Thriller became the Guinness record standard in a year. Also, record companies started really pounding money into artists in an attempt to flash them into sales. Worked for a few others—and still does for one or two artists—but for the most part it was wasted money, and thinking like that almost bankrupted the music industry (before the internet finished the job). It bears noting Prince pimped the sales charts a couple of years ago by having every record he included with his live shows scanned and counted as a record sale. Poof: instant platinum. Soundscan has since shut down that tactic.

MJ +1 Influence, +2 Sales, +1 Business Acumen, +2 Longevity, +1 Live Performance
Prince +1 Business Acumen, +1 Sales

5) MJ helped create the Motown legacy.

MJ was touring before he was ten, then he got picked up by Motown, did as he was told, and the rest is HIStory. Prince was with a major label until he didn't want to be, but there's only one Motown.

MJ +3 Longevity, +1 Business Acumen

6) MJ was one of the best, most original dancers in the world.

Prince has moves (or did before his recent surgery), but we've seen most of them before, eg., James Brown. MJ created moves, most impressively the modern Moonwalk, and at the same time made dancing somehow as important as the music.

MJ +1 Live Performance, +1 Influence, +1 Je ne sais qua

7) MJ continued to push the music video envelope even after setting the highest bar ever.

Thriller is arguably the most lauded music video ever and it certainly created the cinematic feel of modern videos. The video remix? Also MJ. By contrast, Prince typically spent much of his time in videos crawling out of bathtubs and yelling at women in the key of "I'm Naked."

MJ +1 Influence, +1 Business Acumen

8) Prince wrote almost every song he ever recorded.

MJ wrote some songs, but his output doesn't come close to Prince's. Prince is probably the artist most associated with unreleased material, and the bootleg industry owes half of its business to him. Plus, he controls his music, and in key ways has since he signed his first deal. And while his records have dipped in quality overall, there's always that one track that reminds you why he's The Man.

Prince +1 Catalogue, +1 Songwriting, +1 Business Acumen, +1 Longevity, +1 Musicianship

9) Prince has released over 25 records to MJ's 11...more than twice the number of MJ.*****

However, MJ sold over 200 million records worldwide...twice the number sold by Prince. (The lesson? If you want to get paid large, work smarter, not harder. Write nine or ten undeniably hit songs, pimp them all as singles, and sit back for eight years until the elephants in your backyard zoo need some more peanuts.)

Prince +1 Catalogue, +1 Songwriting, +1 Business Acumen, +1 Longevity, +1 Musicianship
MJ +1 Sales, +1 Business Acumen

10) Prince is proficient at a frightening level on multiple instruments.

He played almost all of the instruments on not only his records but some of his side projects as well: the first Madhouse record? The Time? Prince.

Prince +1 Songwriting, +1 Live Performance, +1 Musicianship

11) Prince wrote more incredible songs.

MJ spent time picking the right songs, but he rarely wrote them. Prince is writing a song right now about this essay, and it will be sexy and classic. Prince probably has one album for every classic song MJ has.

Prince +1 Songwriting, +1 Musicianship

12) MJ's personal life imploded well before his death.
Prince is a bit of a lady-chaser, but that's about as bad as it gets. MJ? I don't think I need to even run that laundry list of personal travails off. And when he tried to explain himself it just made matters worse. In fact, it's so bad I have to deduct points.

MJ -1 Grown Folks' Business, -1 Je ne sais qua

13) Prince maintained a strict self-discipline and work ethic to ensure his personal and professional longevity.
There is an anecdote some old bodybuilder had about Arnold Schwarzenegger, where he said that Arnold was so intense when he worked out that a bomb could go off in the gym and he wouldn't even notice. Prince comes off the same way: intense, controlling, makes you sign contracts to not talk about him. Sure, it can be weird sometimes, but it's self-preservation for a lonely man. MJ? Eh, didn't handle this one so well.

Prince +1 Grown Folks' Business, +1 Longevity, +1 Je ne sais qua

14) They were both Jehovah's Witnesses.
Who cares?

15) MJ mismanaged his money.
Let's be clear: MJ wasn't BROKE broke when he died. He might have had some trouble maintaining the lifestyle he was accustomed to, but he wasn't going hungry. He had to cut back to something like two private jets and three homes. Maybe he sold a giraffe or something out of his private zoo, but that's about it. Still, it made him look ridiculous. By contrast, Prince is a voracious businessman, flipping his work into a variety of

platforms: computer games, online music clubs, specialized iPods, books, films. Almost none of this stuff is any good, but you had to buy it to find that out. He even sues his fans with some regularity. I get the impression the man has money stuffed in his mattress…and that's a big mattress.

MJ -1 Business Acumen
Prince +1 Business Acumen, +1 Sales

17) Neither of them has that friend who will tell them, "No."

Aside from having wardrobes ripped out of the pages of Nuts Clearinghouse and Zipper Haus, that they never appeared on the same song—ever—is just plain dumb; two weirdoes so damned navel-gazingly off-kilter that they couldn't sit in the same room for five minutes without sending shivers down each other's too-tight pants. This is when you need a good friend to pull you to the side and say, "Hey man, this would be a really cool thing. Neither one of you need the money. Get over yourself and do this." Quincy Jones wasn't the guy to get it done (though he did get them in the same room), but someone should have pushed harder on both sides…like Michael Jackson and Prince. Someone should have compelled them to make this happen. Understanding that neither of these men were from Earth, a good friend could have.

This is a stone cold draw of zero.

18) MJ was performing and selling Top 40 hits before Prince even had a record deal.***

Period.

MJ +1 Sales, +1 Longevity, +1 Catalogue

19) Prince has written a nearly incalculable number of songs for other artists.

Prince +1 Catalogue, +1 Longevity, +1 Sales, +1 Musicianship, +1 Business Acumen

20) Prince created other stars.

The Time, which most notably gave us Jimmy Jam and Terry Lewis, who in turn recreated Janet Jackson and went on to write about 500 songs that have hit #1. They should be sending Prince Christmas cards in June.

Prince +1 Business Acumen, +1 Catalogue

21) Prince has controlled much of his musical career since day one.

Prince +1 Business Acumen

22) Prince is too stiff with access and public use issues, to his detriment.

Suing fans is always bad for business. Plus, MJ loved attention and money and rights largely unconcerned him because he was so freakin' rich.

Prince -1 Business Acumen

23) Prince has consistently outranked MJ critically, and with more albums.

MJ is essentially historical for one record, but known for three notable ones total. Prince has no less than five critically acclaimed and inarguably classic records, and I'm being conservative here so I can use the word "inarguably".

Prince +1 Catalogue, +1 Musicianship, +1 Songwriting
MJ +1 Catalogue

24) Prince turned his career around; MJ tried, but failed.

MJ's personal life would never allow him a full recovery of his career.

Prince +1 Je ne sais qua, +1 Business Acumen
MJ -1 Grown Folks' Business

25) MJ bought and sold the Beatles catalogue.

Prince had to fight with his company for decades over the output of much of his own material.

MJ +2 Business Acumen, +2 Grown Folks' Business

26) Prince advocates heavily for artist rights and independence.

Prince +1 Influence

27) Prince turned down Guitar Hero.
Prince thinks kids should learn how to play guitar, not games. That's not only a bad business decision...it flies in the face of reality. It would expose a whole new generation to his music, and in a time when many schools are cutting music programs, this goes a long way in generating appreciation. Also, it's improved the sales of real instruments. When was the last time this man was in a music store?
Was MJ even asked for at least Rock Band?

Prince -1 Business Acumen, -1 Influence

28) Prince wears his influences plainly; MJ seems cut from whole cloth.
MJ worked as hard on his image as he did his dance steps and albums. Prince did too, but you can see a lot of previous artists in Prince: Jimi Hendrix, James Brown, Sly, etc. His unique sound and sheer musicianship raises him above much of this, but when you stand MJ next to Prince, the King of Pop almost seems to come from another world.

MJ +1 Live Performance, +1 Musicianship, +1 Je ne sais qua, +1 Business Acumen

29) Prince has never been arrested. Michael? Uh, yeah.

MJ -1 Grown Folks' Business

30) MJ was hands-down weirder.

Prince -1 Je ne sais qua
MJ -2 Je ne sais qua

31) Both of them have unique voices, unmistakable for anyone else.
Even when backing up other artists (Rockwell for MJ, Sheila E. for Prince, et al.) you can see their fingerprints at the scene without even dusting.

Prince +1 Musicianship, +1 Je ne sais qua, +1 Songwriting
MJ +1 Musicianship, +1 Je ne sais qua

TOTALS
Prince "The Purple One" = 37 points
Michael "The King of Pop" Jackson = 35 points

Wow. MJ really messed up in the Grown Folks' Business section, son. This balances out realistically, as he became known to a whole generation of people for things that had nothing to do with music. While his career was powerful enough to sustain his place in history, history is always happening, and he was making it in all the wrong ways at the end.

The other implication here is that when Prince dies, the world will feel it worse than they do MJ. This isn't true for every part of the world, but it might be true anyplace that holds a premium on self-responsibility and loves a good slow jam. Prince is probably responsible for more babies conceived than any other artist in the world. That's greatness.

NOTES
* Both of them had the bestselling record of their careers between the end of 1982 and the end of 1984. *Thriller* was released in November 1982 and because of a "mild" (by MJ standards) first single, "The Girl is Mine," the album didn't really pick up steam (again, by MJ standards) until a little bit later, when "Billie Jean" was released as a single. So for all intents and

purposes, this record "came out" in early 1983.
** Not counting compilations.
*** Not counting work with the Jacksons/Jackson 5.

PAISLEY PARK IS IN YOUR HEART. AND MINNESOTA. BUT MOSTLY IN YOUR HEART.
(2016)

(This was written in October of 2016 after my second visit to Paisley Park, and my first time inside the gates. - sew)

Before April 21, 2016 every Prince fan had a secret. It was the same secret for every fan, no matter where the fan was. Some of us blabbed the secret to anyone who would listen, but some of us tucked it deep into our throats. We did this, not because we were good at keeping secrets, but because we were embarrassed by the secret. It was a silly secret, a secret most of us had no business possessing because we knew better. It was an unrealistic secret, more of a fantasy, really. Now, almost six months after Prince has passed away, the secret has morphed into a regret, for some a howling chasm of despair. The secret was simple, almost elementary in its design.

The secret was this: Every Prince fan assumed that they would one day get to meet him face to face. This wasn't a dream. This was an assumption.

Now, most of us were pragmatic. We knew that we were unlikely to ever end up in a place where Prince would appear, given our rote and plebeian circumstances. "This thing called life," as it were. Prince was never going to show up at our job between concerts, or pop into the McDonalds you go to every day to pretend your lunch hour isn't just another sixty minutes your job is sucking away alongside the other eight. We knew that if we were ever going to meet him that we would have to make the effort, to take the extra step. We knew our chances were greatly improved if we could just get to where we knew he was most of the time, where all of the magic happened. That's where Paisley Park comes in.

We knew we'd have to get inside Paisley Park, his massive studio complex and residence, filled to the top of its industrial white walls with sexy dreams and enough unreleased music to choke Billboard's Top 100 list in any given year (a worthy goal). Every true Prince fan has wanted to get into Paisley Park since the paint dried on the parking space lines back in 1988.

And then in April, there was no more need for the secret. Rather, there was no longer a path toward realizing it, a million bucket lists suddenly made confetti run through a million heart-shaped shredders.

There is a looseness to much of the music that Prince composed after the creation of Paisley Park, though "composed" perhaps renders an inappropriate distillation of his process. The music of *Musicology*, *Diamonds & Pearls*, *The Gold Experience*, *The Black Album*, *Graffiti Bridge*—pretty much most of the stuff released after 1988—leans heavily into band arrangements, sporting jam session sensibilities that having unfettered access to a pristine and customized space affords. After the creation of Paisley Park the music shifted from songs that were composed without concern for whether or not they could be recreated live ("When Doves Cry" doesn't care if you can play it or not) to band music. It is music you invite people over to play with you, to figure out in the air of timeless freedom. Paisley Park isn't a recording studio in the traditional sense. If a studio can be a kingdom, Paisley Park is that land. With its production guts buried in an enormous windowless complex it's easy to get lost in casino time, losing track of what time or day it is, what the weather outside might be. We've made a lot of noise over the years about Madonna's penchant for reinvention, but how impactful were her personas and guises? Prince created palates that did not exist before he realized them. He recorded music that denoted whole shifts in eras. You don't have nasty '90s R&B without "Darling Nikki," and an entire generation of singers chasing its lessons, and the same was true for "Lady Cab Driver" before it, and "Do Me Baby" before it. I don't know what they would have been singing about in 1994, but it wouldn't have been jeeps and slow jams.

After Prince died, the buzz about what would happen to Paisley Park was immediate. The company that oversees Graceland was brought in to set up Paisley Park as a museum, which was more or less in line with Prince's wishes. One wonders at what point in his life he began establishing the building as such in concrete terms, and how close what's there meets that vision. In any event, it opened for public tours this past weekend, then suddenly stopped operations as the Chanhassen city council decided it wasn't comfortable with the amount of traffic and safety concerns that come with the level of tourism such a site was likely to generate. As of this writing the city is allowing twelve more days of tours to happen, and no one doubts that the organizers will be able to navigate whatever conditions are set before them to open the space full time.

Even in death, Prince gets what he wants.

I had been to Paisley Park a few months ago, a detour on another equally amazing trip I can only recount off the record, and stood outside the gate. I expected to write about the experience almost immediately, but the words wouldn't come. There wasn't enough there to write about, or rather, what was there was clearly missing something. The moment was a memorial, but too impersonal. I brought everything to that moment because I had to. The experience wasn't official, and it wasn't Prince. Prince was not speaking through the gate. There was no exchange. Also, his death wasn't worthy of his life and, still trying to wrap my head around that, the right words simply never came. I needed to go inside—to make the secret real—and I believed that, eventually, that day would come.

That day was this past weekend, the second day Paisley Park was open to the public since his death.

I was planning to go on one of the tours later in the month after it had been open a few weeks, but notable social critic and hip hop radio legend Jay Smooth hit me up and asked if I'd be interested in going when he was going to be in Minneapolis. Needless to say, plans got changed. We were to be joined by food writer, sustenance smuggler, and all-around awesome person Tamara Palmer. I was adorned in my commemorative Charlie Brown Still Misses Prince shirt, we had amassed our little purple crew, and Paisley Park siren-called to us over a chilly autumn Chanhassen sunset to come take a peek behind the curtain. While Paisley Park wasn't going anywhere, it was beyond cool to be one of the first people to get inside, two days after it opened (and nearly closed, and then barely reopened just long enough to avoid my having to eat a plane ticket). So this trip almost didn't happen, save that Prince knew what was up. As far as I'm concerned, Prince asked me to be there for the express purpose of telling you something about the experience. I'm going to walk you through the tour in my unapologetically biased and fanboy manner. My impressions will not be objective. As I have written elsewhere, I did not hold Prince in my mind as some distant celebrity, but as a friend who was notoriously hard to get on the phone and who was really bad at checking his email. Also, I sprang for the VIP tour, so I may recount more detail than people who have taken the general admission tour.

(And really, what's with those people? I don't know how you get the chance to go inside Paisley Park and you don't spring for the VIP ticket. It's only a hundred bucks (for now). And while I get that general admission is a fraction of that—$35—how you gonna' come that far and not go all the way? I fear for those people's discounted souls.)

A shuttle picks us up at a parking garage and takes the back road to Paisley Park. I know it's the back road because I drove there before; it's a straight shot when you're not trying to mollify your suburban neighbors. Either way, I wondered if the places I saw along the way were places Prince frequented. Did Prince go to that movie theater? Did he ever pop in to that Jimmy Johns? Did Prince ever fill up at the gas pump I'm using right now? Is that the Walmart where he picked up his prescriptions? Everybody in Minneapolis has a Prince sighting story, an anecdote in which he shows up and hides in the balcony or has a special table or bought some records. It's not unreasonable to think that over the course of thirty years of Chanhassen living he didn't stop into the Speedway once. And once you commit to that law of averages in your head, it's almost like he could still be anywhere, might still peek out from behind a limo window or breeze by on his bicycle.

Upon arrival, people are milling about the front, taking pictures of the lighted entrance and the cubist architecture. We take all the pictures we can now because once we pass into the foyer photos are strictly forbidden, evidence of such resulting in a permanent ban from the premises. Paisley Park had been open for exactly one day and already people have been banned for life for taking rogue pictures. The mind boggles at the logic at play there. It's not exactly a cost prohibitive adventure so anyone with a burning desire to see the inside will eventually get to. Al Roker did a field report from inside the complex earlier in the week for the Today show. He went in some spaces the VIP tour doesn't even get you, so what's the real benefit to being the cat who took a picture knowing you'll be banned for life? How could you allow yourself to risk being banned for life from Paisley Park? What if they do something cool there later and you want to come back and can't? If I actually carried a phone I'd happily let them bag and lock it (which is what they do with your phone until the end of the tour). I didn't want to court suspicion (or risk temptation) so I let them hold on to my tablet, which they didn't have a provision for, so I ended up leaving at the desk with my name written on the back of a discarded receipt. Not the safest transaction, but if my tablet had gotten stolen in Paisley Park that was almost an anecdote worth the aggravation. "Yo, Paisley Park ate my tablet! Prince killing my Candy Crush score, son."

I am initially struck by how small the space seems, even with its high glass pyramid ceilings. It's not really small, just smaller than it was in my head. It's mansion small, and mad colorful (it used to be all white). The entryway is lined with silver, gold, and platinum records and cassettes from around the world, all snugly protected by plexiglass thicker than the shields in any carryout I've ever been in. It's almost cute to see a silver award for *Purple Rain* cassettes. "Hey, you sold two hundred thousand tapes through August 1984, Prince. Congratulations!" Ha. Give it a few more months and they'd be upgrading that Maxell to platinum. During the week after his death he sold 4.41 million albums and songs and had five albums in the top ten of the Billboard 200 chart. Some artists—artists you love—never have an album in the top 100. Some never make the chart at all. Prince put five old ones (back) in the top ten at the same time. That is the first time that's ever happened since they created the chart. Even in death, Prince is still setting records, begging the question, how gone is Prince really?

Stairs to the second floor are roped off and groups are corralled into the atrium proper, where you really start to get a sense of being in the middle of Prince's world even though you just got there. Off to the side are small rooms dedicated to early albums, sporting looped videos, wardrobe and a few choice instruments from the time periods, but not much else. Across the atrium is the "Little Kitchen," which is less a kitchen and more of a break room. There is a coffeemaker and an espresso machine, a refrigerator, a couple of diner booths and a loveseat facing a television. There are some extra blankets to add to the red one already draped there. Thanks to the Little Kitchen I also now have to watch *Divergent* because it was on top of a stack of DVDs next to the TV. Thanks, Prince…?

Much has been made in the news about the decision to showcase his ashes in an urn in the atrium. My party discussed this before we got there, wondering if it was something they should warn people about ahead of time. In person, it wasn't as affecting as I imagine they painted it in their planning meetings. Some people cried, of course, but for most it's a curiosity. What ashes are on display are tucked away in a small model of Paisley Park behind more glass, which was supposed to be poignant but seems almost too small a gesture. The display would probably have had more power at the end of the tour than the beginning, especially since it wasn't opened to showcase its inner details. It just looked like an architect's rendering, not a memorial or shrine.

More chilling—and not a feature of the tour guide's spiel—was the oddly cut section of wall to the side by the front staircase. I kept looking at it, trying to figure out why such a design decision had been made, a seemingly random jagged series of cuts in the drywall. I considered that it might be a secret door (we would see a couple along the way) and shrugged it off as roughshod contractor work until I was able to review video of the area from previous on-site interviews after the fact. The reality is more jarring: it's where the designers have blocked off the elevator where Prince's body was found. I'm glad I didn't know that ahead of time, since I probably would have just stood there staring at the wall while the tours kept passing me by. The "urn" wasn't without its power, but it was devastating to think of how close I had been standing to where he had been found, where his spirit divorced the world, where the music and the soul of it ceased. Covering it up was not a good call; it was the only call. There are people who would have run crying out of the building if they knew what was behind the huge framed pinwheel of *Musicology* concert tickets masking the new construction. Right out the gate the tour inadvertently—perhaps unavoidably is a better word—puts you closer to him than most of us were ever going to get. If you believe in places of power, it's hard to consider it anything but.

The tour guides (who, as it turns out, don't know much more than any real fan) make a point to keep telling us that most of the rooms are as Prince left them, which I found strained credibility upon entering "his" office. The office has a desk and some chairs and is decorated nicely enough, but I know he has one on the second floor near actual residence areas that probably got more use. There is a short stack of books on a table, a few of which are about Egypt. They have a cute conversation piece on display: a suitcase propped against a wall. The docent for this area informs us that it's filled with DVDs, which is odd, but not outstanding. Prince loved movies. There are DVDs scattered here and there throughout the tour, more movies than books, and there are televisions in almost every room. Also, the office features the first cat carrier sighting.

Entering the video editing suite confirms that Prince is not only black, but 1970s black. Mirrored walls and closet doors abound, carpet is everywhere, black and glass is the palate, and there are more afrocentric metal sculptures and wire music note hangings. I don't buy the "untouched" rooms sell they keep giving me, and little things like that make me feel like I'm not too far off the mark. There is a secret door here—one I didn't see coming in, so actually secret—which our guide tells us was full of videos and that no one knew was there until after he died. Pretty sure that second part isn't true, but I roll with it. I got my Encyclopedia Brown on, testing my sneaking suspicion by noting that, while there are two framed movie posters hanging in this room (*Metropolis* and *Bird*), there's a wall with a conspicuous hanger and no picture, and wondered if our host knew what had been on that wall. He didn't, but assured the group that whatever it was, Prince had determined it needed to be empty. I was going to need the training of these guides to tighten up a little because I'm pretty sure no one bought that. Prince has every other wall in the building accounted for, but in the editing bay he took a picture down and left the hook up? Not buying it. Put something on the wall and amend this part of the speech, Paisley staff. Also, another cat carrier. Seeing tiny cat carriers in his more private areas is somehow endearing and hilarious. Now I want to know the cat's name, where it is, who's loving it now, if it actually liked Prince or if it was, you know, a cat.

As we started to move into studios, first B then A, things got more on mission. Considering Prince spent much of his time in those rooms, these were the places I felt more like I was supposed to be. The actual engineering booths were off limits, but you could peek through the glass and get a sense of how he spent day after day, creating, and how the space affected his work. The designers have at least situated a few fake candles and sheets of notes around to make it look Prince-glazed. Standing in these studios—posing with his piano for a picture (VIP), playing on his ping pong table—you get a real sense of how these high quality spaces designed to bend to one's creative will. In one studio a dedicated space for piano is lined with granite, in another it's wood for drums. Despite assumptions to the contrary, there isn't a wall filled with guitars like some kind of musical armory. The studios seem rent-ready, not Prince ready, and a well-placed sheet of handwritten lyrics doesn't change my impression of that. The tour group was treated to snippets of an unreleased song he had recorded for a jazz album he was looking to release, and it's a great song: funky, playful, and slathered with groove…better than anything on his last couple of albums. I could have done with more of that. I could have done with a new song in every room, really. Now THAT would drum up some repeat business, and it would generate a real sense of resonance with what Paisley Park represented: artistic freedom. You couldn't get any closer to Prince now than listening to unreleased music in the room where he made it. That's practically a religious experience, and one they should capitalize on, not because it would make them money, but because it would make the museum the kind of place I have to imagine Prince would have wanted it to be: a place that made people happy and excited and appreciative of the work that went into his art. So the beginnings of a win/win, really.

There is no Paisley Park without *Purple Rain*—the movie and the album— so I had high expectations for a room dedicated to that part of his career, an era that cemented his place in music for all time. The *Purple Rain* room used to be a dance rehearsal studio, and still feels like one: the far wall is still mirrored, the rest of the room is still white, and there's a small control booth by the entrance that I'm reasonably sure has been gutted. The room is still a little unfinished in the corners. The room contains a whopping six items: one of his coats, his Oscar, one of his motorcycles, a bound copy of the script, the electric piano he played, and one of his guitars. Contrary to rumor, this isn't a room that plays the movie on loop; it plays a smashed montage of clips on loop. At this point in the tour I determined that the organizers were either stingy, greedy, misguided, or all three. As museums go, it's got a long way to go: there's not much information here, and while I appreciated seeing what I saw, I knew there was so much more that could have been displayed. The room is huge and swallows up the bank of items in the middle, to the point that it makes these high powered items seem small. There should be three times the amount of stuff in this room as there is. You shouldn't be able to get through the Purple Rain room in three minutes. This was a bit anti-climactic, an exhibit they could have put in a mall or a local gallery, not sold as a museum exhibit.

The rooms that followed are dedicated to two of his other films—*Under the Cherry Moon* and *Graffiti Bridge*—were equally underwhelming. A movie poster, a single outfit, maybe an instrument. I mean, *Graffiti Bridge* was filmed inside Paisley Park. They couldn't roll out something more significant than a couple of items in half of a room? The missed opportunities were starting to mount and I felt myself slipping out of fan mode and into critic mode, which was not the plan. Parts of Paisley Park seem modest in their construction: murals that are in fact wallpaper, frayed edges on pieces here and there. Some of the wardrobe pieces expose an assembly line's care. This is not to disparage Prince or his things, but to more fully realize the man behind the icon. If you had to play fifty shows on the road you'd need some back-up trenchcoats too, and they wouldn't all be pristine. And my god, how small the outfits are. It's one thing to know he was diminutive, but another to see an iconic outfit that was splayed fifty feet tall on cinema canvas (and thus remained fifty feet tall in my mind) on a mannequin the size of my twelve year old niece.

After a jaunt down the Hall of Influences (a mural Prince had done years ago featuring artists he helped build up and artists he was in turn inspired by) and a hallway of awards, we were led to the infamous massive soundstage area, which was draped entirely in black. This is the largest space he would perform concerts in. Now it contained five raised platforms featuring items dedicated to various tours. The exhibits were still stingy—a few outfits and a key instrument from the tour (a signature drum set or piano)—and was swallowed up by darkness. The saving grace of this space was the video montage they had running of live performances, played through the house sound so loudly that you were able to get a sense of what it was like to be there when he performed live. I watched the video for a while and let the space work its magic. In that moment, I was almost overcome with all of the things that I had missed about my friend, and how close I was now to what he had embodied. And it's kind of cool to see video of him playing an instrument that's now less than ten feet away from you.

From the soundstage you step next door to the NPG Music Club, his personal nightclub in a box, which might be the coolest space we came across, and coincidently, the least manipulated by museum hands. It's ready for a party right now, and with the music blasting and the lights all dimmed, all I needed was for someone to hand me a drink so I could get my wallflower on.

Having walked the halls of Paisley Park, I feel like the world has gotten him wrong on the recluse tip. What is it we're all working toward? Retirement? What happens when you can retire at 28 and all you want to do is make dope music? When you can build a complex that encompasses everything you like to do? Who needs to go to a concert when you give the best concerts in the best space, invite the whole city, know they'll pack the joint, and can release a video or album of the show the next day? When all time is studio time? When you can create without interruption, without checking in, without asking for time off? When you can look in a room and say, I made *The Black Album* and *Batman* there, then put it in your basement for years and everybody knows you did that? Why go to a club when the best club in town is yours? Prince would say in interviews that he didn't subscribe to time the way other people did, and Paisley Park conveys a real sense of being out of regular folk time and space, while not holding you at a rich man's arm length.

After his passing, Wendy Melvoin said, "When you create you can speak to him." What about when you're where he created, where you're not sure, somehow he is still creating? What does Paisley Park say back? As I write this, feverishly, I am creating. Let me tell you what Prince told me: that I'm working hard enough, but not living hard enough. That I can have whatever I want in life, but I'm going to have to kick a billion asses to get it. That money can buy happiness, even time, but those things are going to expire before the money runs out, so spend wisely. That I shouldn't be so hard on squads and the people who love them. That immortality can be a drug, but the crash is always fairly human and mundane. That the best advice you can get is to shut up and listen, even when it sounds like no one is speaking. These are things I knew but, doing the work of a good friend, Paisley Park reminds me of. They are things it reveals to me about myself, pushing me on a course from Prince's too-small death to his enormously large life.

Through all of this I realize how selfish some of us have been. Prince could only accomplish what he did as we know it with Paisley Park. It takes many thousands of dollars per week to run a place to enable an artist to do what he did, which is almost every album since *Sign o' the Times* and the thousands of hours of rehearsing, experimenting and producing he did otherwise. We railed against his tightness over his catalog and the dearth of his internet presence, his legal team shutting down every video as it popped up. Yet you can see every dime and byte of it squirreled away in Paisley Park. There's a reason why people aren't touring the homes and landmarking the sidewalk outside of 99% of artists' homes. For everything Prince had, he deserved more, and I dare say better. I'm not saying I'll never buy another bootleg, but I'll feel really conflicted about it now.

Before you leave the interior of Paisley Park there is a section of preserved fence memorials (not actual fencing from the property. Don't go looking for a jailbreak hole in the perimeter). It is laid against a wall where the curators have kept some of the graft fans have left outside. I recognize some of the pieces. They picked good ones, but it's far from representative. The fence was an enormous and beautiful thing that we all knew couldn't last. At least someone recognized the value in displaying a sliver of it, since some of it just ended up in the mud.

The way out leads you, of course, through a gift shop that's really a tented area that was parking before. There are racks of gear from his most recent tours and a few general Prince-themed bits. I considered walking out of there with the internet-generated meme shirt of "This could be us but you playing," which sports the iconic pic of Prince and Apollonia on his motorcycle, smiling, ready to dance and ride and make love to one another in Minnesota barns. And then I thought of her in that moment, what she might make of all this, but then she doesn't need the tour. Any memory she has of him is worth more than anything on the tour. Plus, the shirts run mad small.

I spring for a poster, a bag and the tour book. I also prepaid for the Prince's Favorite Foods sampler plate, which is a veggie offering of various entrees. Something tells me these were things he might have tried, but weren't on the regular menu. My man ate Doritos; I saw him. Ain't nobody spending 12 hours in the studio fueled by kale chips or that orange breakfast of champions, squash. Still, get it if you go. It's probably not canon, but it's got some good stuff on it and it's only $12. We all tried the dessert offerings and agree the Rice Krispie/chocolate/peanut butter treat is a winner.

Walking out of the tented area you find yourself back in the music-less night, an ecstasy exciting your skin, the sadness of concrete welling inside of you as the ocean crash of nearby traffic escorts you back to your un-purple life. You take more pictures of the same exterior you shot when you arrived, but now it means something else. This is the post-coital version, the morning after shot. The little bushes have new meaning now, and the walls look less like industrial siding and more like canvas. You want to rush home and make something, to create, to be glad for what you have. And to blast some Prince music with new appreciation and insight.

Flying home, the fog I got lost in driving to the wrong airport terminal lies over Minneapolis like a rumpled comforter beneath me. I am going home, somehow full and empty at once. All of the creative neurons in me are firing, as if sipping from the water fountain in the NPG Music Club I have tapped into a fount of youth and creativity. I typed the first two thousand words of this essay with two thumbs on the way home, totally forgetting that I was supposed to be terrified of flying. I went to my friend's house and missed all of his parties, forgot where he kept the spare key, smelled the candles already blown out, didn't get to honor any of the favors I said he could call upon me for. Elvis left his building, been gone a long time. But Prince? You couldn't pry Prince out of Paisley Park with a crowbar-shaped exorcism.

If you're a fan, you should go. There is a magic to the place that the tour guides can't convey, though they've been trained to try. If you are an artist of any stripe I command you to go. If something doesn't click on inside of you after walking through Paisley Park (and just the meager half of the complex we've been afforded) then you are no artist. It's supposed to be a museum, but it's not good at that yet. It is extremely good at being an oracle, a place to listen, a place to learn. It should be a library, the loudest library in the world, a library you must dance in for admission. Libraries archive but they also educate. And Paisley Park has just as many lessons to teach as it does memories to impart. Getting in the gate feels like an accomplishment—and for longtime fans, it is—but whatever you get out of it after that genuinely hinges on whatever you've brought in your heart. It's not just a corny-sounding line in a song; that part of the titular song is real. Knowing that makes you wonder what else Prince said that sounded weird was just him recording what he observed. Even in death, Prince stays magical.

EVERY PRINCE FAN
IS THE WORLD'S BIGGEST PRINCE FAN
(2017)

The only reason I'm not a lifelong Prince fan is because I was born before he had a record deal. I was seven years old when he released his first record, and I can recall the exact moment a little more than a year later when I discovered the wondrousness Prince had to offer even in his formative years. I was nine. I broke into my brother's bedroom to go through his record collection, and found the record that would change my life. I've recounted this experience before in greater detail than I offer here — exactly one year ago, to be precise. Suffice it to say that Prince has been an influence on me ever since. And this was back when his records were new, not reprinted as hip vintage swag, so we're talking about a substantial relationship here.

If you're reading this, you likely have your own Prince origin story. The ending to all of them is that every Prince fan thinks they are the biggest Prince fan in the world. It is why encounters with fans are sometimes challenging: You can't tell us anything about Prince, let alone anything that would make us change how we feel about him.

That's an important distinction to make when talking about Prince: Almost no one over a certain age has an impression of the music and not the man. Perhaps, like Jaime Foxx's comic routine about meeting Prince, we all got caught gazing into his eyes while watching *Purple Rain* and pieces of him broke off in us. People have as many opinions of Prince as a person as they do his music. It's rarely just: "I liked *Purple Rain*." Instead, it's: "Prince was a trip. You remember when he had his pants cut out the back at the awards show? Dude was a trip." We can point to other artists we talk about this way, but if we're being completely honest, none of them crossed the cultural lines that Prince crossed with the same success.

More than perhaps any artist in mainstream music, Prince charted a course toward true cultural solidarity. More than that, he succeeded at making that solidarity as close to a reality as art has ever brought us as a society.

Consider race, and that it is not enough to be black in white spaces, even if you are exceptionally talented. Being able to dunk a basketball or play guitar alone doesn't make the space welcoming or diverse or nurturing. You have to, in some way, become an example of what is possible. And so Prince's music and gender and messaging and band all fed into the point: that love can fix every problem we have. Or at least allowing the freedom of any kind of love that could be had to come your way, and to offer it to anyone who asks.

It wasn't enough to preach it; Prince had to exude it. We had to be convinced that, somewhere, someone was capable of expressing all the angles necessary to convince us that such a world was possible — that someone was capable of actually being from such a place. To this end, Prince endlessly integrated his bands, continued to tie the religious to the secular in every inch of his art, and built a complex — Paisley Park — that essentially acted as a mythical Shangri-La, where all the magic was created and spilled from, and which, with his death, has become a weeping wall, where we come to see the temple and leave our thanks. (And where a musical celebration is going on right now.)

Prince took it upon himself, quite literally, to create such space, first within the twelve inches of each plastic disc of musical, and later anywhere he was. It is why his concerts, perennially sold out, were populated with all manner of people from multiple generations. The swaying grandmother next to the wild teen, the assured gay next to the pompous Christian, all of us singing the same (sometimes naughty) lyrics as if the world might really come to an end if we don't get our acts together in this song.

In death, the dynamic persists. Anywhere his presence is summoned, the air changes a little: The men become softer, the women sexier, the androgynous more glorious, the cursing less rampant, the politics more gray, and everybody becomes a little less self-conscious about what they've got on, understanding that Prince always wore whatever we could possibly be wearing better. Your hair, your shoes, your dress, your make-up — all better with Prince.

Prince fans operate the same way any other type of fan operates. Very few of us are degreed musicologists, approaching new albums with the slavering drill of an academic. We instead attach distinct and personal memories to songs: where we heard them, what we were doing while we listened to them, who we were with, what we thought of them. But if you note a singular gleam in the eye accompanying Prince recollections, that's not a coincidence. When Prince was really cooking — 1981 until 1987 — every line of music he touched seemed to be coming from another dimension, some place that sounded similar to ours, but got twisted coming through the wormhole. It was easy to attach memories to songs like "If I Was Your Girlfriend" or "When Doves Cry," because they didn't sound like anything else you'd ever heard, radio or otherwise. Half of every memory attached to a Prince song starts with "I had to stop what I was doing because I couldn't stop staring at the radio/stereo/television."

I say this as if I am not one of them, when in truth I am no different from my enthusiastic kin. I can pretty much name every first-time Prince listening experience from the beginning. As I grew in my fandom, the set-up conditions of a first listen were usually tantamount to a ritual: The volume had to be just right, nothing else could really be going on in the room, and I certainly couldn't do it with other people around. I had to be able to listen without reservation, to cheer — sometimes physically — on the winning parts, rewind the parts I couldn't believe I was hearing, curse the bad parts, and otherwise come to my own conclusions.

Today, on the first anniversary of his death, a new "album" of previously unreleased work was slated to come out, entitled *Deliverance*. Because I am not an ordinary fan, I acquired the album (technically an EP) a couple of days ahead of the release. I did nothing nefarious or complicated; it was there for the listening, and despite how anyone, including Prince, feels about bootlegged material, Prince has always been a little too tight for his own good in this regard. All that was left at that point was to listen to it.

It had been years since I'd needed to observe the rituals. Even when he was alive, I had let the first-listen ceremony slide on his last handful of albums. He hadn't put out a record I could stand behind since *Musicology*, and that had been well over a decade ago. Fortunately I'm not some slavering fanatic, so the number of stations in my first-listen process are few: Alone? Check. Phone off? Check. Ready to take notes? Check.

At a scant sixteen minutes of material, it's not a lot of new music, but it is enough. Containing tracks that bootleggers hadn't had their way with yet, it was a genuinely refreshing listen. I review it elsewhere in depth; in short, it is a perfectly acceptable epitaph. It's essentially a gospel musical, or rather, it is six songs made into a musical by their compilation. It is a good record — a better record than he has put out in some years. I imagine to the point of certainty that the experience I had listening to it was the effect he wanted his music to have at this stage in his career: uplifting, spiritual, compelling you to bond with others through the dance of life. It is unmistakably Prince, and because this is how he has always opted to speak to me directly, it is like seeing my old friend again.

And yet, he kept this music to himself for the last ten years. And, as it turns out, may have never intended to share it.

As of this writing, the album has been snatched back into Prince's storied vault, the conditions of its release not having passed legal muster. I have mine, but millions of listeners do not. There is a sadness to that math, but more importantly, there is a chaser of bitterness for me. What does it say about Prince that he had a set of keys to salvation — by his definition and on his terms — and chose not to unlock the door? Chose instead to give us *Planet Earth* and *3121* and, beyond all reason, *LotusFlow3r/MPLSound*? In my mind, a real friend would have pointed out this travesty to him, but then, Prince was not known for surrounding himself with people inclined to criticize.

Once again, much sooner than anticipated, I can tell you where I was when I heard Prince music I had never heard before. It was three days ago in my basement, early evening. I was wearing jeans, no shoes, and was on the tail end of a cold. That all sounds fairly ordinary, and it is, but it all happened in a different world than the one I have listened to every other Prince album in.

It is a world wherein I know Prince isn't squirreled away in the bowels of Paisley Park at all hours coming up with something in response to what's passing for civilization these days, or more selfishly, trying to change my life again. It is a world where genius has a bar that it will not rise above again. It hurts knowing that on the nights when I am slaving away at my own projects that I cannot convince myself into another hour of work by remembering that my lifelong-but-distant friend is probably doing the same thing at the same time. It is not a world any of his songs has prepared me for. One year into living in this world, I find it infinitely lessened by his presence, catastrophically full of itself and nowhere near as cute as it thinks it is.

I await new conversations with my old friend. None of them will be what he would have said given the chance, but what he had to say was so powerful, so touched by genius, so profound in its ethics, that he may change my life still. If he has a legacy besides the spotlight and gold records, it is in the sum total of what he has yet to say, and for that I'm all ears.

TO ALL THE PRINCE I DIDN'T LOVE BEFORE: REVISITING ALBUMS I DIDN'T DIG

As much of a Prince fan as I may be, I didn't like half of the records he put out. I'd like to think that makes me discerning, but it probably just means I'm old and don't like change. Except that isn't true. I found enough Prince material after the greatest hits parade he was leading for the whole of the 1980s to keep praising his talent. *20Ten, Crystal Ball, Diamonds and Pearls, N.E.W.S.* and *Musicology* were solid records to me when they came out. And yet, with a catalog as vast and storied as his, a reevaluation is sometimes in order, especially after the bookend of his death.

Again, I didn't like a lot of records, but I just picked a few here to revisit. The first is one I get asked to address a lot. The others are self-explanatory.

The Rainbow Children (2001)

I had a real beef with this album when it came out. It was so close to being a good record I found it too frustrating to revisit more than a few times since its release. In recent years, I have befriended a lot of fans whose opinions I respect who claim that this is the record that turned them on to Prince. One friend was so adamant that I revisit it that she ordered me appropriate incense and candles to set the mood for a proper reception of the album's merits. It's a religious record; it deserves something of a ritualistic treatment. The request wasn't very left field for me. I used to make similar arrangements when I listened to Prince albums for the first time back when the expectation was that they would be good and savored upon playing.

I also had an issue with this record because it was being billed as a "gospel" record of sorts, but it did that in theme only; the music wasn't gospel, or easily definable at all. Which would have been cool if that meant it was breaking ground like *Parade*, which it did not. And really, by the time this came out I was getting tired of Prince trying to sell me on his takes on religion. This album always had that just-found-church energy to it, which, if you've ever had a cousin who just got out of prison and found Jesus, you know is kind of annoying.

Anyhow, I lit the incense, fired up a candle, and settled in for the ride.

"Rainbow Children": A blues groove I have to admit is better than I remember. In all fairness, the blues have taken on a much more powerful vibe in my life as I've gotten older, so this definitely speaks to me in a way it didn't seventeen years ago. I might even like this song now, especially with the groove switch in the last third of the song. That's some Zappa feeling right there, almost a "Shut Up and Play Your Guitar" mood (albeit still way more reserved).

"Muse 2 the Pharaoh": A harmless smoothed out groove with some harmless scat and even some bearable rap. My problem with this originally was that it was too harmless and it had a rap section and I just could never trust Prince when it came to rap. I knew he didn't respect it as an art form, so his attempts to incorporate it flattened out its appearance in his work for me. That said, by the time *Rainbow Children* came out he had smoothed out some of the rough edges and by 2001 he was doing it in a way that didn't make me hate him so much. I don't need to play this song, but I definitely see why people dig it. Also, I think it's funny that someone who held on to as many conspiracy theories as Prince did is talking about how other people's superstitions are suspect.

"Digital Garden": The slowed down voice thing is already wearing me out.

"The Work Part 1": This was, and remains, a solid funky number masking its zealot messaging. I dug this back then and still do, though when I want funky Prince I go to other stuff.

"Everywhere": This has a solid choir-backed groove I didn't give a chance back in the day because I was turned off by the blatant religiosity of the lyrics. I like this more than I did, but the bar was pretty low.

(At this point in the record I recall that, in 2001, I was losing steam because it was clearly a jam-based affair and I wasn't partial to his jam-based stuff. In later years I developed a mildly shady respect for that phase of his catalog, as there was more to compare it to as time passed. All of which is to say, at this point in the record I'm way more forgiving, as this foray is better than a lot of the stuff that came after it.)

"The Sensual Everafter": Somebody call Santana and tell him we found his groove. This (essentially) instrumental is cute. It has shades of "Alexa de Paris," which is always a good idea, and the sliding bass works despite itself. This is kind of a SpyroGyra type of thing that could go either way. It's aged well, let's say.

"Mellow": We get it: you really like smooth jazz. Oh, hey, Najee. At this point in the record, the mellow vibe is starting to grate a little, which is kind of the opposite of what mellow is supposed to do.

"1+1+1 is 3": Prince isn't fooling anybody with this fake funk. Sure, I like the ear candy of the "Irresistible Bitch" synth pops and guitar squeals making an appearance, but the groove isn't very genuine here. It sounds like a 2000s era Prince cover band.

"Deconstruction": Yawn.

"Wedding Feast": Wait, I thought we just had an interlude. This lightweight choral skit is wack. Totally took me out of the record. Now I need more incense.

"She Loves Me 4 Me": This one I've actually played in the last 17 years. It's a fine song that's kind of stock, but with enough Prince flourish to make it work. So this one breaks even. It definitely sits in the right place on the album because it needed a shot in the arm here.

"Family Name": If you think Prince never owned a Frank Zappa record, this track should dispel that notion for you. The robotic intro is straight *Joe's Garage*. This is essentially three minutes of skit and sampled noise leading into a Sly Stone (see the title) riff that's too referential to match the strived-for intensity of the too-long intro. This is one of those songs that you know Prince was thinking, "We're going to wear this out live," which was true, but on record is too tight to make me move much. I do wonder if he paid for the Martin Luther King, Jr. sample. Probably not. I don't think I've heard of an instance in which Prince paid for a sample, despite numerous appearances of them.

"The Everlasting Now": Something that circles a traditional gospel song, but stops just short in light funk territory. This song is how you know you're supposed to listen to all of this together: it only shines in context. Take this song out of this album and play it along with twenty other Prince jams and you won't remember it was played. In any event, Prince liked it well enough: it showed up in tours for three years, well after this record was out. He probably should have shaved a couple of minutes off of this on record and saved the eight minutes version for the live show. Also, if you had any doubts about his contributions to The Time records, that's all in here too, albeit nowhere near as legitimately funky.

"Last December": Ending the record on a loping rock note featuring Larry Graham on bass for no other reason than because why not, this preachy song is a feel-good ditty that ramps up halfway through, then dives. It's like listening to a bird flying in a hurricane; it has too many peaks and valleys, but whatever. He's going to make sure you get all the grooves he had left over on the cutting room floor. You can definitely tell when John Blackwell is on the drums. He kills on this track in the power groove parts.

"Last December (Reprise)": It ain't over, saints! Hidden track time, which, for the record? Totally not worth the wait.

Overall: Upon a more recent review, I have to admit that this record went up a few notches for me. I was apparently really bucking against his religious message at the time, but see how it informed his decisions on this record in a way that wasn't just shoving a new manifesto in my face (*Lovesexy*, *Emancipation*). I might even sneak some of it onto a list for someone who was into smooth jazz or progressive gospel. Its funk largely falls flat, but it stands as a solid testimony to Prince's ability to craft a compelling narrative arc.

The Love Symbol Album (1992)

To say I was not a fan of this record when it was released is an understatement. It came out on the heels of *Diamonds and Pearls* (1991), which Prince had waged a full-scale campaign to make a hit record: TV appearances, interviews, the whole nine. When he started dropping singles off of this album I was still burned out from the previous record, which was okay, but wildly inconsistent. I wasn't recovered enough to receive another so-so record.

This album hurt my feelings for several reasons:

1) I felt like I had been lied to.

There were two releases before the album dropped in October: "Sexy MF" and "My Name is Prince." "Sexy" was a good song, but "My Name is Prince" was a jam, albeit spoiled by Prince's interpretation of a rap palate and overproduction. When the rest of the record didn't live up to the potential of these two tracks, I was incensed. He even made them the first two songs on the album, so I really had expectations. Silly me.

2) Prince was really deep in his rap phase.

It was no secret that Prince was not a fan of hip hop. In an attempt to show us crotch-grabbing kids (who did we learn it from?) what real music was, he decided to swab this record in hip hop sensibilities, thus proving the theory that you cannot honor well that which you do not respect. Anyhow, let's get into it:

"My Name is Prince": This has a strong hook and the bass programming on here works, which is why this single was acceptable. His rapping was weak, but it's Prince, so of course it was. The song is way overproduced, and in 2018 reveals itself for the relevancy stretch it was. This track is full of mistakes from a hip hop production standpoint, and you can tell it's done by someone who doesn't listen to enough of the right kind of rap to get good at this. The producer of this song listens to chart rap, and chart rap alone. The only smart thing about this song is that it was released after "Sexy MF," which was a much better song and extremely well received at the time. In 2018 this just sounds like a C+C Music Factory outtake.

"Sexy MF": Prince acting his age, thank you very much. He's still toying with rap lyrics here, but it's in his wheelhouse thematically and sonically, so it works. This still slaps sixteen years later.

"Love 2 The 9's": While not a bad song, I remember why I didn't like it: it kicked me right out of the record. All of a sudden I wasn't getting the same Prince at all, but a Prince I knew, which was just confusing. Since shock isn't a factor now, the song stands up better, and is a fine song. Still not dope, still not bad.

"The Morning Papers": Didn't like it then, still don't like it. I got nothing against power ballads, but this one is so straight ahead that it's boring, which you should never be able to say about a Prince song with this much guitar soloing.

"The Max": No.

"Blue Light": This reggae out of a can track is more confounding than anything else. Why are we doing this? I just couldn't think of a reason why Island Prince showed up for work that day. Nobody called for Island Prince. If the song was going for something political or genuinely Jamaican, I might feel different. As it stands, even now it's still just canned world music that happens to have Prince singing on it. It feels like a mash-up strictly because the bpms match, not an earnest effort to say or play anything new. This song is beneath Prince.

"Wanna Melt With U": Oh god, who invited Rave Prince to the party? This was trash in 1992 and it's decomposed into a fine silt in 2018. This album is starting to feel like a producer's beat demo. "See? I can do everything (poorly)!"

"Sweet Baby": A saccharine slow song that doesn't groove enough to become a slow jam. So by the numbers it's boring.

"The Continental": Someone take his hip hop sample pack from him. That he tries to butch this song up with rock riffs just makes it sound like a mess. Still.

"Damn U": Around the time this album was out, black music was really pumping out the slow jam. Radio was loaded with ballads and grinds and basement party slow drops. The trend was so pervasive that when I was talking to Roger Troutman of Zapp fame at the time, he asked me what songs of his I liked and when I mentioned a slow jam (probably "Computer Love"), he replied, "Yeah, all everybody wants is slow jams." I thought (but didn't say), "Well, your slow jams are really, really good." Here, Prince actually takes a risk for the time, since it is a slow jam, but it doesn't sound like the rest of the field. It's a torch and lounge take on a slow jam, and because it's him, it works and you're not mad it exists because you expect him to bring something a little different. It's when Prince tries to do what everyone else is doing that we have problems.

"Arrogance": You know from the synth bass upfront this song is going to be bad news. This song is like a Reeses cup if you replaced the chocolate with shit: you have to cut through the parts that are wack to get to those hard workout breaks in the middle. And by the time you figure out what's going on, the song ends. Just wrong.

"The Flow": Prince's idea of a hip hop song also includes the word "nigga," and this song features the first time he puts it on a released record. That's the only outstanding thing about this otherwise trash rap song.

"7": A classic. I've never been a huge fan of this song, but listening to it now I have a new appreciation for how it infuses a hip hop production value (that bassline is basically Lowell Fulson's "Tramp." Or, if you're not that old "Salt N Pepa's "Tramp," which is also Lowell Fulson's "Tramp") without being a rap song.

"And God Created Woman": This should have showed up earlier in the record because by the time I get to it here, I don't care that it's not an entirely bad song. The religiosity of it is kind of jarring at this point on the record, but it's all just a mess anyway, so who cares.

"3 Chains of Gold": Nobody loves this song more than Prince himself. He made a movie out of it, a comic book, and this not-great song. It's like he dropped a showtune capper into the middle of his rap record and it just makes no sense. Taken by itself, it still befuddles and honestly, brings nothing new to the table. Everything in this record we've heard on a more coherent track before. It's a bad pocket opera that owes no little bit of inspiration to Queen's "Bohemian Rhapsody." Hated it then, and time has not improved its station.

"The Sacrifice of Victor": This might be the most frustrating track on this whole album. Prince gives us lyrics that are surprisingly personal and politically revealing, but they're entirely buried in a horribly produced rap song with gospel aspirations. There is a nice acapella thing happening at the very end that probably should have informed the whole song, but alas.

Listening now, the record has a couple of accidental hits that probably wouldn't hold up for a new listener, while the rest of the record is a straight no. The record meant certain things to Prince at the time, but sixteen years later it is more of a curiosity than it is a listenable record.

Lotusflow3r / MPLSound (2009)

No. Some things even I won't do.

I don't think I hate a Prince record more than this one. In fact, this might be the only Prince record I actively hate. The other ones I "don't like" I simply don't like. I wish them no harm. But this collection of misses? I abhor. There will be no revisiting because the report will just consist of curse words I strung together to meet a word count.

Piano and a Microphone 1983 (2018)

Clarification: I actually like this release. I just don't think it should have come out when it did.

What Prince would have wanted released after his death is a losing battle out the gate; nothing released after his death that consists of vaulted material would appear to meet the criteria of what Prince would have "wanted." That said, this release isn't remotely in the spirit of something Prince might have released at all. At the same time, Prince wasn't always his own best counsel when it came to what people might want or should get.

Since his death, much has been made of what Prince would or would not do regarding how his work is handled, or more specifically, how it is monetized. To say that Prince music has appeared in numerous projects prior to his death is an understatement. IMDB lists almost 250 instances in which a Prince song has been used to score a film, TV show or sports event, and not just in America, or even in English. And while many teeth have been gnashed over the use of "Let's Go Crazy" in a recent Capital One commercial, Prince established a publishing arm, NPGMusicPublishing.com, as recently as 2014 for the express purpose of monetizing his catalog. The press release that went out on April 4, 2014 includes the following statement:

> *NPG Music Publishing is now actively seeking placement for some of Prince's best-loved songs in film, television, video games and the commercial realm. Rolling Stone has called Prince "One of the most naturally gifted artists of all time," and now the world will be able to experience and enjoy more of his music through a myriad of mediums.*

The part about video games is telling. Online video game journal *Gamestop* reported in 2009 in an article titled "Prince Kissed Off Guitar Hero Deal" that the artist said in an interview with Tavis Smiley:

> *"Well, I ain't mad at them. I hear it made, like, $2 billion and they came to us and offered us a very small portion of that," explained Prince. "But I just think it's more important that kids learn how to actually play the guitar. It's a tough instrument--it's not easy. It took me a long time, and it was frustrating at first. And you just have to stick with it, and it's cool*

for people who don't have time to learn the chords or ain't interested in it, but to play music is one of the greatest things."(Gamestop, 4/30/2009)

The most revealing part of that statement is the second sentence, the part where Prince mentions how much money he discovered a game like Guitar Hero generates. That Activision's offer was too small is the lede here, not the music civic lesson that follows. That's all stuff you say when you don't want to make it look like you can be bought or that money isn't a factor, which was both very true of Prince at times but ultimately not enough for him to pull the trigger on dozens of projects that would actually make that a reality. Five years later, he forms a publishing company that, on day one, hung a shingle stating he was open for licensing business. Fans may not approve of the appearance of a Prince song in a credit card commercial—and it is likely that he wouldn't have approved of it either— but the suggestion that Prince would never have approved of commercial usage of his music is worse than myopic. It's wrong.

Bottom line: Nothing after Prince's death is likely to be something he would have done. He may have, at best, approved of a particular end result, but not released the project left to his own devices. If he wanted to release albums or videos he certainly had the means to do so. He almost certainly thought he had more time, and there are so few instances of him reaching back into what he has done before that the assumption that he might approve of any project formed from his mountain of unreleased work is probably wrong. The man simply did not have a desire to advance his artistic agenda on the back of previous work. Every other artist could do that, but that's almost entirely why Prince wouldn't. Sure, several retrospectives came out before his death (four to be exact), but outside of the b-sides disc of *The Hits* collection, those were concerned less with legacy and more with the fact that it was a way he could still go gold and collect the check that comes with the numbers.

So here is what I propose: I move that we end all criticism of a new release of Prince work that hinges on his likely disapproval and focus instead on the merits of the project itself. His disapproval of any posthumous project is duly noted through common sense deduction moving forward. Let us instead focus on whether or not new projects add to or diminish his legacy.

THE TOUR THAT MIGHT HAVE SAVED PRINCE'S LIFE
(2018)

One of the perks of spending an ungodly amount of money to attend the second annual Celebration event at Paisley Park was getting to watch footage from a January 21, 2016 performance (set two) of his *Piano and a Microphone* gala event. He did two performances that day and they were pretty much trial runs of the tour that he was preparing to mount a month later. It's not the last performance of his life, but it's within three months of it, so there's a lot to unpack for listeners, primarily because it was a tour unlike any other concert Prince had done in nearly 40 years of live shows.

The Piano and a Microphone tour was strictly as advertised, featuring no band, no wardrobe changes, no elaborate staging or lighting cues, no backup dancers. He didn't have to dance or stand, eschewing entirely the brutally physical performances he was famous for, save for those fleeting leaps when the spirit of the moment moved him to walk away from the piano, sometimes for real, sometimes for effect. There were no grueling day-long rehearsals or hours-long soundcheck jams. The massive and expensive infrastructure that marked his shows was entirely absent from this tour.

There is a humbling that comes with seeing how good he is at playing piano, and at the same time realizing how little we mention this in comparison to his guitar playing. He could have done a tour with a guitar and a microphone, but he chose the piano. Prince is a phenomenal pianist, but he is a god on guitar, and he knew this. He could have sold out all of the same shows on his chief instrument, and he knew this too. Yet, in the spirit of challenging both of his audience and himself, he opts to tour on piano. He does this not so much because he wonders if he can do it, but because we do. Well, not me; I knew he could do it. No one has seen Under the Cherry Moon more times than I, and this is outside of the weeks I spent trying to learn how to play "An Honest Man" from a static-riddled cassette. I'd pay good money I don't have to watch Prince play piano for an hour and a half, anywhere, anytime.

Warning: math ahead. Prince does twenty shows in eleven dates, starting two days after Valentine's Day until mid-April. Even at two shows per day (except for two dates, when the shows were in larger venues), they were spread out in leisurely fashion: a couple of days in Melbourne here, a few days off, then a couple of days in Sydney, and so on. He was only on tour for elven days spread out over two months. This after a year of doing no proper tour at all: the 22 days he did perform in 2015 weren't part of a tour; they were just one-offs. 2015 was the Prince equivalent of taking a year off. While twenty shows in two months sounds like a lot of shows in a short amount of time, it's a schedule with a far less rigorous load than any other tour he did since he began touring in 1979, and with significantly lower stakes than any tour before it. At the point in his life at which he conceives of the *Piano and a Microphone* tour he only needs to tour for rent money on Paisley Park or fun, and the way it was designed catered to both, as well as his declining health.

The rhythm of the shows allowed Prince ample time to connect with audiences in a direct and complimentary way. There are times when attendees become the drummer or back-up singers. Prince's engagement is infectious and cajoling, especially when he chides the audience for getting a common lyric wrong. He frequently plays with a rolling, heavy abandon that isn't present on his records. I have heard it before in bootlegs, where he noodles and pounds an idea into being. It is when he is most himself, when he is searching, and he brings that aspect of his process to the fore in these shows. There is an undeniable glee in having bottled the joy of just—and finally—being himself.

Playing the shows seemed to recharge his body and spirit, or at least not take him to the point of exhaustion, even when moments of sadness or a memory best recalled alone reared their heads. He seemed able to channel that energy into a more resonant performance, digging deeper into a new take on an old song or riffing in the way he often composed, through purposeful twiddling and jamming. The first day of the tour was especially telling in this respect, opening in Melbourne the day after his former lover and protégé, Vanity, passed away. He dedicated a couple of songs to her early in the show, and after having seen footage from the gala a month before, I find myself amazed at his strength in that moment.

I have to mention one performance from the gala in particular to bring this observation home:

There is a point during the gala performance of "Sometimes It Snows In April" where, halfway through the nineteenth song in a twenty-four song set, he hits the line, "Sometimes I feel so bad, so bad." The "so bad" is sung with such earnest that it made everyone watching the video dab an eye or outright weep or get up from a chair or hug whoever was next to them. Or all of the above. He riffs on just those two words for thirty seconds. In those thirty seconds is a clear and subjective interrogation of suffering and pain that, when weighed against what we now know about his health at the time, has to be one of the most revelatory instances a Prince audience has ever been exposed to. He can't even finish the lyrics, opting to vamp into the more upbeat "Dear Mr. Man." Unlike so many other times in concerts, this self-interruption is real, has a meat and bones ache to it. That we know he dies (and under what conditions) not long after this show was recorded drives the knife in white meat-deep. It is a gut-wrenching rendition of a Prince classic, and it is the only version I ever want to hear for the rest of my life. Nearly a thousand of us—almost as many as had seen it when it happened live—sat in the same room where the show had been practiced, performed and recorded, and at movie screen size it was if he was with us again. And once that hits you, you cry again.

Painter Jackson Pollock once said, "Every good painter paints what he is." Read in this light, the *Piano and a Microphone* performances are perhaps the most purely Prince displays ever. He is at his most vulnerable and honest, his most challenged and challenging, at the height of his considerable powers while stripped of his traditional arms, and unburdened almost entirely of expectation. He has come to play in every sense of the word, and he takes to the task with relish. If you ever wondered what he heard in his head as he composed, these shows reveal that. If you wondered where his breaking points and crossed lines were, they're present as well. And in the sharing of so much of himself, it is possible that Prince would have finally discovered a new kind of adoration, a love that reminded him that his audience was capable of seeing him as he was, as a person and not just a dancing, shrieking rock god. We no longer required the accoutrements and fanfare. Just sit with us, shoot a joke here and there, and play whatever you want. And in the relinquishing of all that old baggage—the costumes, the flashing lights, the grueling rehearsals, the weight of carrying a hundred people backstage every night on your name alone—he may have found a new peace, a new way to carry himself, a new way to be.

The *Piano and a Microphone* tour might have been more than the greatest Prince tour ever; it might have been an experience that saved his life.

WWPD: WHAT WOULD PRINCE DO?

I spent a lot of my life waiting for things to happen to me so that I could better understand Prince songs. What's a jockey got to do with Corvettes? I wondered at eleven years of age. Who are the leaders of the new breed, or for that matter what's a new breed? What exactly is an *accu-jack*? I didn't learn what every reference on the *Controversy* album meant until I got to college. By then I could check grown folks books out of a proper university library, and for the first time engage women who could see themselves clear to experiment with a young man in possession of an enviable Prince poster collection hanging in his dorm room. The irony is that, in my rabid quest to uncover such secrets, I pretty much ended my college career before it even began. When people ask why I was expelled from the Ohio State University after only two quarters, I tell them I was immature. If I trust them, I tell them the truth: I was trying to live up to various Prince lyrics.

As I got older, Prince's influence remained a constant in my life, though those lessons were increasingly falling into cautionary tale territory instead of the goals box. The influence wasn't all-encompassing or something I felt compelled to put a name to. Eventually I settled into, nothing as blasphemous as a religion, but a philosophy that seemed to get me over the occasional hump in a relationship or in the event that I had to make a difficult decision. I would simply consider what Prince would do in a similar situation.

I have been operating under this philosophy before I put words to it. For years, I would be working on a project or a poem, stop, and think "What would Prince do?" and something resembling an answer would show up. As manifestos go, it's not bad. I have an almost 80% success rate when applying the right follow through to that question. In the instances in which I was a little off the mark or things didn't go my way, it was usually because my interpretation was wrong, not the mantra.

WWPD is not meant to be interpreted literally. At no point in my life has a problem come close to being solved by buying a pair of heeled boots and leaping from a piano. It is an independence-based principle, and independence is something I've struggled with over the years. One of my three fatal character flaws is a natural inclination toward groups in everything. I've come a long way in recent years, and considering what Prince would do in a given situation remains one of my most frequently accessed tools of choice in combating this flaw. There was a time when, whenever I came up with an idea for a project—say, an album I wanted to record or a poetry event I wanted to do—I would immediately ask myself who I should get to participate in it, even when it was something I'd proven capable of carrying myself. Eventually things got to a point where I struggled to even process ideas without input from others, which evaporated my will to execute anything beyond what I had to do, which in turn made me resent those duties. Finally, exhausted of purpose, drive, and patience, I asked myself "What would Prince do?" I knew enough about Prince's work habits and personal predilections to gather something like an honest answer, which in this case was "Prince would turn on the tape machine and play all the instruments." Through enough application of this Socratic self-help school of thought, I learned to do the same in my relative situation. I turned on the tape machine and played all the instruments and things got done.

There are people who knew or at least worked with Prince that could find exceptions to the conclusions I drew over the years. Prince wouldn't actually do that, sir, they'd offer. The beauty of the WWPD question is that the answers don't need to be absolute to be effective. They need to be goals, and when it came to goals, Prince was pretty good at sinking the shot: win all the awards, make all the money, turn out all the shows, build the entertainment complex, gain control of the masters…those are back-to-back three-pointers from half-court going in.

Here were some moments ripped from the headlines of my life in which the WWPD rubric came into play:

Dilemma:

Before my high school career was three months old, a girl I had slept with told me she had gotten pregnant, and I felt the need to immediately tell my mom. My mother was angry, but suggested I ask the girl a few pertinent details because the circumstances sounded fishy to her. Turns out mom was right: the girl was lying and I didn't know nearly as much biology as I thought.

WWPD?

Try to do the right thing and take on the responsibility, regardless of his age, but then, upon uncovering her caprice, give her all manner of hell. ("Baby," "I Hate U")

Dilemma:

I was dumped by a girl that I adored and was inconsolable. The grief was making it impossible to move, to start my days, to be creative or funny or social.

WWPD?

She's dead to him. Take as little time as possible to get her out of his system, and not let the sun sit on thoughts of her. ("Another Lonely Christmas")

Dilemma:

My boss was constantly tripping and likely racist.

WWPD?

Clear his throat, announce he's quitting, call up a lover, and take a day trip into the nearest rural area. And, of course, have sex. ("Raspberry Beret")

Dilemma:

I saw an ex-girlfriend several months after we'd broken up walking with another guy (multiple times).

WWPD?

If the new guy was underwhelming, puff out his chest. ("Free")

If the new guy was an upgrade, sulk all the way to the gym or a nightclub. ("Something in the Water (Does Not Compute)")

If the new guy looked oddly like him, chuckle at her obvious attempt to replace/not replace him, then wish her well. ("Purple Rain")

If she acts like she didn't see him, rejoice. She petty and she played herself. ("Baby I'm a Star")

Dilemma:

This homework/manuscript/project is due tomorrow and I'm not even close to done.

WWPD?

Prince didn't sleep much. He would get to work. ("Let's Work")

Dilemma:

About to consummate a first-time moment with a new lover, it became clear that she was way more versed in the ways of love than I was.

WWPD?

Take note, but go for it. Give it his best shot. Enjoy the ride. ("Little Red Corvette")

Dilemma:

Maybe it's me, maybe it's you, but this relationship is not working. (Multiple times.)

WWPD?

There are times when I can't do what Prince would do, not because I'm not rich or god-level talented, but because what Prince would do was wrong. Seeking advice or solace from a Prince song is one thing; knowing how he dealt with relationships in the real world is another. When in doubt between the two, I default to what I know of the man, not the art. All art is, on some level, untrue. So hitting up Prince for relationship advice was always very hit or miss. Prince was a control freak, and while that can be a useful trait to apply to a project or piece of art, it's a disastrous way to navigate people. He had terrible luck with long term relationships, and I'm convinced he and I would rarely line up on what to look for in them beyond the physical. I had enough toxic masculinity to drill through in my own upbringing without adding his power plays to the mix, so I've always tended to relegate Prince's relationship advice to mixtapes and days when Sade is too much. Also, for a guy who was always getting laid while at the same time constantly singing about how badly women treated him was kind of weak, or an irreconcilable dichotomy. Prince could capture the problem with your relationship, but he couldn't show you the way out of it, and gave horrible advice in this regard. ("Strange Relationship")

Dilemma:

A too-young girl expresses that she has a crush on me.

WWPD?

Again, sometimes Prince is an example, not a guide. He liked his women young, and more than once younger than anyone around him should have been comfortable with considering the way the relationships were developing. Grooming was a real thing with him several times, always just on the right side of legal, but not something you would have abided by if it were your sister talking to a rock star on the phone for hours. Mind you, it shouldn't matter if it were your sister, but politically we're not at a point as a society where we are applying this kind of line-skirting equally. And part of that is because it remains so common, particularly among celebrities, to the point of expectation. There is evidence enough to suggest that these plays were more about power and controlling the inexperienced than a sexual predilection for young women because they were young. Long story short, your response to the question of how young a given potential paramour was before you became an item should never be, "We didn't do anything until she was 18."

("Hot Thing," "The Morning Papers")

Dilemma:

I can't get my team to do this work.

WWPD?

Prince did not settle for less than what he envisioned, nor suffer people's inadequacies. If you blew a performance or said the wrong thing or didn't come when he called, you either heard about it in no uncertain terms or you would never hear from him again. That said, he was notorious for giving random people important jobs that they had no experience in. Most people believe this was so that he could retain as much control over them as possible, since it's hard not to follow orders when the gaslighting starts over whether or not you were ever qualified to be in the building. At the same time, when you've convinced everyone you can play every position, it keeps them from getting too comfortable with the job.

Dilemma:

Every time we talk we fight.

WWPD?

Prince frequently recorded a song where a conversation would do. ("Bob George," "Man o War")

Dilemma:

I'm not sure what my next move should be.

WWPD?

Go crazy. ("Let's Go Crazy")

THE FUTURE OF PRINCE
(2018)

Following Prince's death, questions immediately began circulating about what would become of his work—released or otherwise, but especially otherwise—and how his legacy might unfold now that he was no longer here to guide it. Two years after his death, there are still more questions than answers.

Every new legal development involving the estate invites speculation from Prince fans, headline skimmers, and everyone in between. As new albums of previously unreleased material begin to make their way into the market, the machine of social media devours and attempts to contextualize Prince for the future, or at least the next couple of days as interest holds. The sun will forevermore rise and set on a Prince song. At any point on any clock, somewhere on the planet a deejay in Japan or a single mother in Detroit or a teenager learning how to play guitar in Mississippi will put on a Prince song for pleasure, answers, or solace (or all three if it's *Around the World in a Day*). Prince isn't going anywhere, but one wonders what his stay will look like.

To this end, I have some predictions. I've broken them into a few general categories: The Music, Fans, Research, and Paisley Park.

The Music

Of all the predictions I'll make, this is the easiest one.

While there will never be a new Prince song written after April of 2016, there are hundreds of Prince songs yet to hear, and most of them will be new to anyone who isn't a moderate to hardcore bootlegger. If we read into sales of posthumous releases (which hardcore fans will purchase regardless of the content) then the number of people willing to engage bootlegged work probably number in the tens of thousands. We're talking people who traffic in at least one legally unavailable copy of a Prince album or handful of songs. Sales of the recently released *Piano and a Microphone 1983* came in around 34,000 sales (U.S.) in its first week. It is safe to surmise that most of those purchases were by hardcore fans and some number of bootleggers, anywhere between 50-75 percent. Also using that math, 25-

50 percent of the people who bought the album out the gate essentially bought music that was new to them. As someone who has listened to more than his fair share of illicit Prince material, I envy the person for whom tracks like "Wally" or "Roadhouse Garden" will be new. I am also made immediately weary thinking of all the gnashing of teeth hardcore fans will make that the illegal song they've been rocking for a decade isn't a "fresh enough" release. Music companies don't typically cater to people who are going to buy something anyway. Those are sales you can always count on, and so long as you release a product with low enough overhead, you can't lose money on a new Prince album. Whatever the future of Prince music will be lies in the hands of people who aren't hardcore fans.

With the digital release in the summer of 2018 of the remaining half of Prince's discography that was previously unavailable in any form, there is plenty of music that returning or new fans can access that no longer has to contend with the barriers of time, access or commerce. People who haven't listened to Prince since *Diamonds and Pearls* can now treat themselves to wholly serviceable fare like *Crystal Ball* and *20Ten*. Even if old fans didn't take a break until after the market-friendly *Musicology* (which more people received at concerts as part of a concert package than bought in traditional outlets), that was still fourteen years ago. There's plenty of Prince music to be had since 2004. You may not like it all, but you now have a dime bag of albums with which to figure that out.

Since whether or not to release music at all is ultimately a numbers game for stakeholders, the good news is that any release is still the equivalent of printing money. Even if they didn't want to front the cost of physical CDs (and, keeping it real, a vain amount of vinyl) they could at any point release a digital version of something new and treat physical copies as special releases…like they do with most music now anyway.

It's a safe bet that new Prince albums will continue to be released at an average of one per year. The overhead at this point couldn't be lower since the music simply has to be logged, mastered, and released. The only limit here is the imagination of the estate in what they release.

Alongside these developments, the illegal Prince industry—primarily bootlegged albums and videos, as well as internet content like pictures and usage of Prince music—will continue largely unabated. It will continue to be legally challenged by the estate, but it will continue to have little to no effect. The internet is an enormous and ever-rolling tide. You cannot produce enough cease and desist emails to quell the ocean.

Fans

The future of Prince fandom is harder to predict because old fans will remain fans, but new fans will be pledged with carrying the torch of Prince's legacy beyond the next twenty years. If new fans don't, Prince could be relegated to used music bins and WalMart barrels of random greatest hits collections forever (or at least until CDs stop being a thing). And to create new fans there will need to be adequate champions of Prince's legacy.

Interest in Prince has exploded since his death, but interest is fickle. To turn interest into actual support—or better, culture—content and context must be curated, shared and, in a way, taught. The good news is that people love being told what they should not only listen to, but respect. It's easier to have a random thinkpiece contextualize an artist we don't know for us than it is to have to listen to ten albums without any guidance. As a society we have come to accept, and in many cases, prefer the behavior modification tools of social media that allow information to be downloaded into our brains, but we like having values injected for us even more. It's frightening way to interpret how we seek out and process new music, but it's also par for the course for anyone with a phone in their pocket. The artists and ideas that are championed while providing wide and free access are the ones that will be remembered. Prince has his champions now, but it's too soon to say if that will be the case in another twenty years.

Current champions of Prince fall largely into two categories: mainstream fans who swear by certain eras of Prince but are largely unaware of his deeper cosmology (anecdotes about his cohorts, work habits, "unavailable catalog"); and diehard fans who know and own everything but whose temperament and social skills range from tolerable to get out. Neither of these groups will get Prince across the finish line of history in their current form. The first will die off having given too little too late to the cause, and the second will become increasingly irrelevant as the internet eats away at their stash.

When you consider the state of music journalism these days and the dearth of credible artistic criticism in general, the journals and academic infrastructure that traditionally keeps audiences informed have, in their quest to be branded and hip and young, become something resembling an enemy to the legacies of older artists. It is dangerous to one's audience to say as much out loud, but I refuse to live in a world where Prince has been millenialized. "Oh hey, hi. Welcome to my ironic record collection. I remember when my dad used to play this old purple record on Sunday mornings and wow, what's with that bedazzled overcoat on the cover? That's hilarious." This is the set-up for nearly every hot take on a long-standing music artist because much of the writing about music now is done by people who lack a direct relationship with the music they're being paid to write about.

Prince's legacy isn't a given. It can go away, or at least go away in the way that respectable things go away. Respectable legacies are mentioned but not curated or supported or carried into the future beyond their names. It's like the Harlem Renaissance: everybody gets that they're supposed to respect the art movement, while at the same time being unable to name more than two artists who participated in it. Most schools don't even bother to teach it anymore, and so, very soon, there will be a generation of Americans who don't know what the Harlem Renaissance is. That dip in awareness took a hundred years to happen, but 80 years of that didn't have to contend with technology and its millions of distractions and cultural implications. Without people consistently carrying Prince's standard—not just his music, but his unparalleled showmanship, craft, catalog, and work ethic—there is no guarantee that in twenty years his name will trip off the tongue the way it does now.

Prince could, without mindful, empathetic, and open-minded fans, go the way of the great musicians of the CD rack at gas stations everywhere: ubiquitous, but not present.

Research

I've written elsewhere in this book about the perils of not bearing in mind and cultivating who gets to build Prince narratives, at least culturally, so I won't belabor this point with repeat information. I hope I have adequately conveyed the risks. That said, we must also be wary of how much we project versus how much we know. Those who care about the future of Prince must be mindful of replacing one Prince mythology (a self-curated body of research, analysis, and interpretation) with another (open source theories, subjective assumptions, personal hot takes, facile thinkpieces).

The short, tough love version: We probably have another twenty years to get all Prince stories directly from their sources before all the people who have them are gone or opting not to revisit them anymore. But the problem with getting the stories isn't with people like Sheila E. or members of The Time or Wally Safford or Eric Leeds or dozens of other people who worked with Prince not wanting to tell their stories. The problem is with the people trying to get the stories. We ask the same things over and over. We don't do our research, so we waste what little time we have with our subjects on the same stories. Somehow we have to, very soon, change the people who are seeking the information so that we can get better, deeper, more resonant information; or amplify and make more accessible the deep pockets of work that has already been done. We can't have everybody starting from zero in an attempt to mollify their slice of a random ignorant audience.

Paisley Park

It is impossible to overstate the importance of Paisley Park to whatever impact Prince's work may have in the future. Even with the vault having been gutted of Prince's storied recordings (which, for the record, needed to happen) the complex remains the place where Prince composed, recorded and, in the end, lived. Being able to walk through the studios and spaces Prince occupied is not only informative but inspiring, and with further tweaks and programming additions it could become a place that warrants more than a single visit.

As it stands, Paisley Park is a serviceable museum, if still finding its way. It is a few solid decisions away from being a good museum—they're too tight with the exhibit items and there should be more happening in the studios and soundstage—and several more from living up to its potential as a destination location worth repeat visits beyond choice events for hardcore fans.

The greatest concern is whether or not Paisley Park is sustainable as a museum before it runs out of time to live up to any other potential. At its current admission prices the overhead isn't enough, though they make a regular killing on merchandise. Much like a theater, the real money isn't in the ticket but the upsell. Long-term support also can't come on the heels of what has become something of an annual fundraiser in the Celebration events. There was not enough difference in the schedules between the first two posthumous years and there was a marked dip in attendance, largely suggested by this reason.

Paisley Park's role in the legacy of Prince is unique, and its ideal contribution would be beyond a museum capacity. Paisley Park could be a lot of things: a functioning studio that releases new music as a label (after the Jack White/Third Man Records model), a home for viewing and listening to Prince performances, music clinics, deeper VIP tours at higher rates, reunion shows, dream band gatherings, current artist concerts, a listening library, etc. None of these are unachievable things. They require vision and leadership and a keen eye on what fans are suggesting they will support, which are things Paisley Park can acquire if it does not already possess. The complex is a state-of-the-art facility able to accommodate audiences of various sizes for variable purposes. The estate could be capitalizing on that next week. It's Paisley Park; a certain cache will always come with that name. There is little to no reason why it can't or shouldn't be the last word on where Prince's legacy lives.

There is so much Prince to share, and thousands of people who only have a surface relationship with what he has done, what it all means, and what such a body of work could teach us. Prince's example is real value building that could make real changes in the culture and art we engage. There are real stakes beyond just having a new album every year or so. The infusion of Prince mechanics into the machines of education, technology, entertainment, business, and a host of other fields could offer powerful tools with which to better engage the world around us and each other. Which, coincidentally enough, was what Prince's various new religions were preaching the entire time.

BOOTLEGS, B-SIDES & PLAYLISTS

DELIVERANCE: A REVIEW OF THE ALBUM
THAT ALMOST WAS

Because of the circumstances under which this EP is making its way into the world, I don't know how long it will be available, assuming it makes it to its original release date three days from now. Mind you, no one knew this album was coming out, so to already see it catching some legal heat is hardly surprising. That said, here is what might be one of the world's first reviews of *Deliverance*, track by track.

"Deliverance"
This is the released track everyone can listen to now. It's a gospel/blues scorcher that makes no bones about its religiosity, the kind of track you end a show with, not kick it off. It sounds great, and is a great opener here, thematically. Considering the rest of the record blends as a movement, it's a great standalone choice. I don't know that this would be a great single, but it's in league with some of the stuff on *Musicology*. It would, in fact, have fit that album nicely.

"I Am"
This material was recorded during 2006 and 2008, between two extremely weak records—*3121* (2006) and *Planet Earth* (2007)—and this track sets us firmly in that period. Headed for a markedly rock and jam direction (culminating in a much worse record by 2009 in *LotusFlow3r/MPSL Sound*). Here we get the kind of playing and composition we were hearing in the albums near the end with his last band of public record, 3rdeyegirl: heavy groove rock, but without the pyrotechnics and arrangement choices inspired by trying to sell a new band muddying everything. This is Prince rocking out, but in a club, not an arena. It's a sweaty track, perhaps the sweatiest gospel song you'll hear this year. It is probably the song Prince would have started this album with if it were up to him, but it's not a better song than "Deliverance." If you recognize the chords of "Tambourine" floating around in the mix, congratulations you're either really old or really hardcore.

121

"Touch Me"

Prince taps a lot of points throughout his career in this whole exercise, and this one is very tellingly from the *3121/Planet Earth* phase of his career in tone. "Touch Me" ties back to the previous track in the second half of this basically transitional song. At less than two minutes it's not trying to make much of an independent statement so much as it tries to clear the palate. This is a bit of moving the stage furniture that does its job: gets you to the meat. You start to really notice the musical constructions here: the wandering questioner in an almost bucolic setting, answered by the thundering god of what is to come.

"Sunrise Sunset"

If you didn't know this was arranged like a musical (which Prince has toyed with in the past), this track would totally betray it. The Broadway lead in, the pop piano opera strains, the way the orchestra fields the heavy lifting, the sappy lyrics…straight showtune. It would sound corny if you didn't know it was a set-up for the next piece (which is also straight musical narrative structuring).

"No One Else"

This is the track I keep coming back to. It has nice *Crystal Ball* touches to it: a little spooky, heavy blues bass, some warped guitar and synths, some odd droning…it's a little kitchen sink in all the right way. This has some sounds and production choices I thought he'd given up on, so the ear candy on this track is a lot like getting a call from an old friend you haven't seen since you both walked out of a theater after having seen *Graffiti Bridge*, laughing hard, trying to figure out how that album ties to that movie.

"I Am (Extended)"

This is basically "I Am" again but with another minute or so of jamming to pad it out. The song is good enough that you want a fuller treatment, but it's hardly what I'd call a cap to the movement. The inclusion of this, while welcome, is how you know it's not exactly an above board collection.

In short, this EP is what happens when you let a fan go through the

122

tapes. A fan would almost assuredly make different decisions than Prince would, even within a finite pool of options, and this release is all the better for it. It is impossible now to know what Prince had in mind for these tracks, but the way they're laid out here works and there's no filler here. At a mere sixteen minutes in length it's better than the last eight albums he put out, which is to say it's his best "album" since 2004. Mind you, this was sitting in a room somewhere with no signs of ever being release. This is yet another gold brick in the foundation of his already majestic and mindboggling compositional legacy. And you should get it now before his estate grinds this to dust in court and it just becomes the best mastered Prince bootleg of all time.

HOW PAISLEY PARK CAN BE A BETTER MUSEUM

If the curators had done nothing to Paisley Park it would still be an honor to be there. I know: I was there on day two. That they have modified the space—despite roundly and falsely claiming to have left some rooms on the tour "untouched"—but not amplified much about the experience beyond making you feel like you should feel lucky to be there at all does generate some disappointments along the way. There is something magical about being in Paisley Park even as it is, but for those who are more than the casual fan, there are a lot of missed opportunities. Prince's legacy should thrive in a singular way through the vehicle that only Paisley Park can provide. Here are a few ways the opportunity to tour Paisley Park can improve as an experience (because it should be an immersive experience, not a ham-fisted tour). I sorely want this project to win not only because he wanted it to win, but as someone who cared in a real way for Prince. He changed my life. Being in Paisley Park could have that effect on everyone who walked in the doors if they…

1) Stop lying about the rooms being untouched.

I know you don't mean all of them, but even the ones you're advertising as untouched have been manipulated (and by extension, so have we. Not cool). I'd rather you touch them by putting even more stuff in them. I don't need to see a dirty plate or anything. I'd settle for some insight into his record collection, or some more instruments. The cat carriers are cute, but not canon, yo. We've figured out that cat been gone. Quit trying to play with our emotions.

2) Stop being stingy.

This is my biggest gripe. There isn't enough stuff on display, period. For someone who supposedly had 200 guitars, I think I saw ten. More costumes, more instruments, more memorabilia, more pictures…more everything, please. I had more—and more unique—posters in my dorm room. And why am I seeing posters at all? I should be seeing props, not stuff I already own. Half of these rooms should feel like the junky dressing room in *Purple Rain*. Remember how eclectic and wild that room was?

124

Break out the puppets and masks, yo. Get a little funky with it.

3) Let it be free roaming, like an actual museum.

The guided tours are largely being led by well-meaning but uninformed folks who (sometimes) have better stories when you pull them to the side than the script they have to give. Q&A in some of the areas was painful for super-fans. You've stripped it down to child-safe levels anyway, so you might as well let us just walk around until we see everything. I know you want to get us for a VIP ticket and "extra content," but...

4) Make VIP a real thing.

Being VIP supposedly adds more time on the tour with a professional guide, with the lone photo opportunity being to take a picture with a piano that a thousand people are going to have. Add some real value to this level: access to other spaces, multiple photo ops, access to other unreleased music...you know, stuff you can't just walk into. The tickets are still reasonable to me, but ultimately there wasn't much stopping someone who wasn't VIP from accessing the VIP tour anyway.

5) More music.

If you're on a Paisley Park tour you probably already own most of his music. If we get to go into his studios, we want to feel like we're really in there. The curators already let a little of this happen in one studio, where they play a snippet of a song off of Tidal, and another actually unreleased track for about 30 seconds. The studios are the heart of Paisley Park. It's where the Prince we love did all the stuff we love him for. Amplify this with more unreleased music. It doesn't have to be pristine. We're a thirsty lot.

6) More video.

Considering his private ("untouched!") editing bay is one of the first things you see on the tour, there should be more video playing in general. And not just loops of music videos, but concerts (of which there is some), interviews, and other stuff we've heard about but never seen. There are thousands of hours of footage in that complex. There should be video almost everywhere you turn. One of the stops is in a private watching room. There are TVs in almost every room. Turn the TVs on and let some stuff play as we come through.

7) Get some larger shirts.

Even the XXL shirts were pretty small. I'm sure that's fine for Prince on his off days, but real XXL folks are putting those shirts in memory quilts when we want to wear them.

8) Get some anecdotes from the people who know.

One of the unexpected benefits to opening up Paisley Park as a museum is all of the people who were there over the years while Prince was alive giving insight into aspects of the space that are impossible to glean out of the tour. Was the NPG Music Club really where he partied? Where was the basketball hoop? Where did rehearsals take place, and what were they like? Some video clips of interviews would be nice, and it would cut down on the number of embarrassing Q&A moments between super-fans and tour guides trying to answer these questions.

9) Light the skylights.

If it's true that the pyramids on top of Paisley Park would light up whenever Prince was present, then keep them on. All the time. Forever.

Extra Credit:
– Some *Graffiti Bridge* stuff would be nice.

To be clear: This one makes me feel a little dirty to propose, so much so I couldn't justify it on the proper list. *Graffiti Bridge* was a project whose importance we would all do well to not exaggerate. That said, he created the film in Paisley Park. Talk about speaking truth to power. If there is anything floating around from this film in terms of props you'd do well to put it on display. He put all his eggs in that basket at the time and a jacket is hardly worthy of capturing that effort (assuming everything wasn't chucked into the dumpster after it flopped).

PRINCE'S COMEBACKS: WINS & LOSSES

There were several instances in Prince's career where a comeback was necessary in not only the minds of fans, but Prince's as well. We can debate the results of how he addressed a comeback (in my house he won a few, and lost a few), but there is no debate that even he thought he needed to make a case for himself multiple times. The math:

Comeback #1: *Controversy* (1981)
This one is sort of a soft comeback, and debatable, since Prince hadn't really hit superstar status at this point in his career. He entered music with a very powerful contract with Warner Brothers that signed him for three albums. By the end of his third album, *Dirty Mind*, he was hurting a bit: Warner wasn't getting what they wanted, and Prince wasn't breaking through the way he would have liked. In 1981, Prince buckled down and recorded *Controversy*, which performed well enough to stabilize him professionally and set him up for the slam dunk that would be *1999* the following year.
Score: 1-0

Comeback #2: *Sign O' The Times* (1987)
After *Purple Rain*, a burned out and frustrated Prince rushed out *Around the World in a Day*. While it was respectable enough critically, legions of new fans were turned off by its non-*Purple Rain*-ness. He then tried to compensate for this dip with *Parade/Under the Cherry Moon*, which made matters infinitely worse. By 1987, he needed a comeback not only for fans, but to gain leverage with Warner Brothers, who he was feuding with at the time. He was forced to whittle down his dream project (*Crystal Ball*) from a three LP set to two LPs. This effort yielded *Sign O' The Times*, and it was a win all around, even if it was under duress. He was back on top of the pile critically and commercially.
Score: 2-0

Comeback #3: *Batman* (1989)
Prince squandered his *Sign O' The Times* clout a number of ways (not

touring the US, releasing the wrong songs as singles, etc.), capping his power by aborting *The Black Album* the day before its release, and offering the ultimately frustrating and preachy *Lovesexy* in its stead. In the span of two years he had burned through his goodwill and needed a win again. *Batman* was a slam dunk all around, even if half the album is below average Prince.
Score: 3-0

Comeback #4: *Diamonds and Pearls* (1991)

Prince is the poster child of what happens when you give the wrong person too much power. Every time he makes it back on top, he blows it by acting out. Thanks to the utter failure of *Graffiti Bridge*, a mere two years after *Batman* he needed a win again. This time, however, the comeback required more work and was arguably the first comeback to not hit the mark. *Diamonds* is an okay record with a lot of fluff that had great marketing and was propelled by a more accessible Prince, performing in capacities he hadn't before and doing the random high profile interview. His comeback game was starting to show cracks.
Score: 3-1

Comeback #5: *Emancipation* (1996)

Having freed himself from Warner to put out what he wanted whenever he wanted, Prince again expends more energy making an album succeed outside of the studio than within it making great songs. His press campaign got this three LP record sold in respectable numbers, but in reflection almost all of this collection is fluff. He scraped by on a comeback here, but fans were getting worn out from having to basically foot the bill and carry the weight under so much so-so music. A win, but barely.
Score: 4-1

Comeback #6: *Rave Un2 the Joy Fantastic* (1999)

In the year that was his to lose artistically and professionally, he failed spectacularly. *Rave* was a horrible record despite all efforts, and fan burnout had caught up to him at this point. Only diehards were still going in the paint for him, and the critics bombed this effort on the heels of so many

already bad records in recent years.
Score: 4-2

Comeback #7: *Musicology* (2004)

After years of records that people either didn't like, never heard were released, or came out of Warner against his wishes, Prince returns to the funk and R&B well that made his career (albeit more produced) and a new game plan to stack the professional deck (and pump up his coffers). *Musicology* was something of a return to form, which is an odd thing to say about someone who had inhabited so many forms. By counting sales of the album as part of a concert ticket package, he backdoored his way onto the charts and back into platinum sales, conversely forcing the press to pay attention to him again. It's a pimp move so slick that Soundscan changed the rules so no one else could repeat the feat.
Score: 5-2

Comeback #8: *Plectrumelectrum* & *Art Official Age* (both 2014)

After a number of misfires and general wear and tear on his career, Prince tried to impress again by remaking his band, bringing on a co-producer for the first time, and trying to gimmick us into yet another more-is-better trap, this time releasing two albums on the same day. Unfortunately, both of the albums were extremely weak, continuing a string of misses that general audiences were barely aware of anyway. He hadn't had a gold album in eight years by this time, and these albums wouldn't cross the line either.
Score: 5-3 (I'm being kind by counting the two records as one loss.)

Considering most artists don't get to launch a comeback at all, the amount of times that Prince was able to place himself in a position to take the shot is astounding. It says a lot that he was not only able to get back to the plate so many times, but that he was able to live up to the hype most of their time. And yet, while a score of 5-3 looks like an overall good thing, we have to remember that there are a lot of bad records that made his comebacks necessary. Prince may have been the comeback kid early on, but his comebacks were fading fast and costing more to make happen twenty years ago. When one considers what he had in the vaults, and how good a musician he was every minute of his career, it's a genuine shame that he didn't knock the ball out the park with more consistency.

10 INSTANCES OF PRINCE BEING HILARIOUS
(2014)

A recent Prince single - "Breakfast Can Wait" - is getting renewed attention because it's been released on YouTube out of Prince's camp with an image on its "cover" of Dave Chappelle dressed as Prince from Chappelle's classic basketball sketch. The attention is mostly excited with strains of surprise about Prince's apparent sense of humor. However, any long-term and observant fan of Prince will tell you he's always been a funny dude. Here are ten more examples of His Royal Badness' playful side besides "That ain't Lake Minnetonka":

1. "Wrecka Stowe"
   Under the Cherry Moon is pretty much Prince on comic blast for an hour and a half, but the "Wrecka Stowe" scene is arguably one of the funniest exchanges on film since 1986.

2. The song "Moviestar."
   The early music of The Time, mostly written by Prince, featured vocals largely pre-recorded by Prince, which Morris Day would then redo based on Prince's cues. This song never made it onto The Time's roster, but we'll always have Prince's version, which is pretty much hilarious from beginning to end.

3. Prince stalking some guy on a British television show like a lion.

4. The dog chewing up bags of submitted demo tapes on the old New Power Generation website.

5. The song "Bob George."
   Sure, it's a little rough around the edges in terms of its sensibilities, but how funny do you have to be to be able to say about yourself the following lyric:

   "What's he do for a living? Manage rock stars?

131

Who? Prince? Ain't that a bitch?
That skinny motherfucker with the high voice?"

6. The completely unnecessary cough at the beginning of the extended
version of "Raspberry Beret".

7. Prince's face.
     Prince doesn't do anything candid; every grimace, stare and lip twist
is intentional…and on occasion, he makes some of the funniest mugs of
any celebrity out there. The instances in which he shoots a random pang
of mock disgust or surprise is made all the funnier by the fact that he
very rarely does more than hit you with a Come Hither face. He's probably one of only a handful of people anywhere who practices staring. See
the video for "Kiss" and just about all of Under the Cherry Moon.

8. The song "Housequake."
     A complete James Brown riff gone off the rails, and one of only two
times the Daffy Duck voice filter was acceptable.

9. Kicking Kim Kardashian off stage for not dancing.

10. Prince's 1997 appearance on *Muppets Tonight*.
     I mean, in what world, right? While much of the show is typical guest
star stuff, there is one sketch in particular that really makes you laugh out
loud: the Muppet Hoo Haw sketch, which is probably the only docu-
mented time Prince has ever worn overalls.

UNCOLLECTED BITS AND ASPARAGUS TIPS

THE 4 TYPES OF PRINCE CONVERSATIONS

There are four scientifically acknowledged types of Prince conversations, and before diving into one you to have to decide which one you're in:

1) The Public Noob Conversation

The most common type of Prince conversation. This is the casual or drive-by conversation any two or more strangers can have that references about 5% of his catalog: *Controversy, Purple Rain*, "Kiss," and the time he performed with the butt cut out of his pants. The participants will make no mention of bootlegged or even B-side material, if they are even aware such work exists.

2) The Releases Only Fan Conversation

A conversation with someone who is hip, but primarily bases their conclusions about Prince on his legally released output. This person will know a few Prince stories as well.

3) The Oeuvre Fan Conversation

A conversation with a Prince fan who weighs the sum total of his creative output, bootlegs and all, in their observations. This person will also be fairly conversant in Prince lore outside of his music.

4) The Inner Circle Conversation

You could go your whole life as a Prince fan and never find yourself in this conversation. This is the exchange in which at least one party in the conversation has had some interaction with Prince or with someone who has had direct and notable contact with Prince: a former band member, a former co-worker, etc. This is not necessarily someone who happens to live in Minneapolis and has a Prince sighting story; everyone in Minneapolis has a Prince sighting story.

COVER EGO: PRINCE PLAY TOO MUCH (UNUSED EXCERPT)

While going through Prince bootlegs today, I was reminded that one of the pleasures of doing so is comparing the artistic decisions of artists who cover his songs. Not his hits—no one should be covering his hits really, ever—but the stuff he wrote for other people. His original demos vary in recording quality from rough to pristine, and you either like the songs or you don't, but the constant throughout is Prince. He didn't often write songs for other artists in the way that most people imagine, say, compensating for their range or considering their overall abilities. He wrote Prince songs and then other artists and producers had to make some executive decisions about how to translate what he did. It's why almost every song he gave to someone else always sounded better when he did it, even if the quality of the tape was suspect. (Except for Morris Day's parts. Morris always owned those Time songs.)

The song "Eternity" is a great example. Sheena Easton covered this song in 1987 for her album, *No Sound But a Heart*, and the differences are clear in the first few seconds of the track. The song becomes pure '80s B-side, replacing the demo's odd breathy choir sounds for straight orchestral string backing, and stacking Easton's voice until she becomes a chorus. I get why they did it—the song has religious connotations, so let's go choral—but the whole affair is a bastion of overproduction. Most obvious is the ending, easily the most notable (and best) part of the song: Prince ramps into a soulful riff that floats on a bed of soprano vocal bedding, ending in an almost theatrical abruptness. Easton, shall we say, takes a less challenging approach to the part, and rightly so: She ain't no Prince. His demo catalog is full of moments like that, moments when you wonder what Prince or the other artists were thinking. Was Prince being funny? Was he being competitive or petty? Did he not care about the song or just want the cash? It's almost impossible to know now, but I can tell you that if I'd have been given that demo I'd have handed it back. "Come on, man," I'd say to him, "do you not want to give me a song or what?"

THE ONE SONG YOU SHOULD LISTEN TO OFF OF EVERY PRINCE ALBUM IF YOU'VE NEVER HEARD OF PRINCE

For You—"Soft and Wet"
Prince - "Bambi"
Dirty Mind - "Head"
Controversy - "Sexuality"
1999—"Something in the Water (Does Not Compute)"
Purple Rain—"Let's Go Crazy"
Around The World in a Day - "Tamborine"
Parade—"Girls & Boys"
Sign o' the Times—"The Ballad of Dorothy Parker"
Lovesexy—"When 2 R In Love"
Batman - "Partyman"
Graffiti Bridge—"Tick, Tick, Bang"
Diamonds and Pearls—"Gett Off"
Love Symbol—"Sexy M.F."
Come - "Solo"
Black Album—"Rockhard in a Funky Place"
The Gold Experience—"I Hate U"
Chaos and Disorder—"Dinner with Delores"
Emancipation—"Betcha BY Golly Wow"
Crystal Ball—"Crystal Ball"
The Truth—"Don't Play Me"
The Vault... Old Friends 4 Sale—"Old Friends 4 Sale"
Rave Un2 The Joy Fantastic—"Man O War"
The Rainbow Children - "Muse 2 The Pharaoh"
One Nite Alone—"A Case of U"
Xpectation - "Xosphere"
N.E.W.S. - "East"
Musicology—"What Do U Want Me 2 Do?"
The Chocolate Invasion - "Supercute"
The Slaughterhouse—"Y Should Eye Do That When Eye Can Do This"
3121—"The Dance"

Planet Earth—"Future Baby Mama"
LOTUSFLOW3R—"Feel Good, Feel Better, Feel Wonderful"
MPLSound—"Chocolate Box"
20Ten—"Sticky Like Glue"
Plectrumelectrum - "STOPTHISTRAIN"
Art Official Age—"U KNOW"
HITnRUN Phase One—"June"
HITnRUN Phase Two—"Xtralovable"
Piano and a Microphone 1983—"17 Days"

PAISLEY PARK'S RESTROOMS

Paisley Park has public restrooms, at least two sets that I observed: a pair in the lobby and a pair near the entrance to the soundstage. Both of them are just far enough away from studios that I have a hard time imagining that Prince, deep in a marathon session of recording, would run in heels all the way down those halls to use one. I imagine there is a restroom of some kind connected to the studio behind a hidden panel or something similarly rich.

And then I wondered if, given the opportunity to choose between a stall and a urinal if Prince would default to stalls. I had to believe that someone who was so controlling of his image wouldn't want anyone to happen upon him standing at a urinal, gauging how PRINCE pissed.

And at that point I realized I had gone down a rabbit hole no man should pursue.

TIMES PRINCE USED THE N-WORD IN A SONG

- "The Flow"
- "Bob George"
- "Y Should Eye Do That When Eye Could Do This?"
- "Da Bang"
- "Gold Nigga"
- "2 Nigs United for West Compton"
- "Don't Play Me"
- "17 Days" (*Piano and a Microphone 1983* version)
- "The Sacrifice of Victor"
- "Johnny"
- "Cloreen Bacon Skin"

8 THINGS PRINCE DID ON MY BIRTHDAY (JANUARY 25)

1982—Attended the 9th annual American Music Awards ceremony in Los Angeles, CA. This is also the night that he met Denise Matthews, aka Vanity.

1985—Released the single "Take Me With U" b/w "Baby I'm A Star" in the US.

1985—Played a concert with The Revolution in Memphis, TN.

1987—Recorded horn overdubs by Eric Leeds on "There's Something I Like About Being Your Fool."

1997—Cancelled a concert in Hattiesburg, MS.

2004—Sat in with a house band in Beverly Hills, CA at a Golden Globes after party.

2005—Released a remastered version of the *Sign O' The Times* movie in Canada.

2006—Played at a Támar Davis show in Los Angeles, CA at The Roxy.

* According to PrinceVault.com.

ABOUT THE AUTHOR

Scott Woods is the author of *Urban Contemporary History Month* (2016, Brick Cave Books) and *We Over Here Now* (2013, Brick Cave Books), and has published or edited work in a variety of publications. He has been featured multiple times in national press, including multiple appearances on National Public Radio. In April of 2006 he became the first poet to ever complete a 24-hour solo poetry reading, a feat he bested seven more times without repeating a single poem.

Printed in Great Britain
by Amazon